Kevin Brownlow

The Search for Charlie Chaplin

UKA PRESS

Published by UKA Press

Copyright © Kevin Brownlow 2005, 2010

Kevin Brownlow has asserted his right under the Copyright, Designs and Patents Act 1988 to be identified as the author of this work. This book is sold subject to the condition that it shall not, by way of trade or otherwise, be lent, resold, hired out or otherwise circulated without the publisher's prior consent in any form of binding or cover other than that in which it is published and without a similar condition including this condition being imposed on the subsequent purchaser.

First published in Italian and English by
Le Mani - Microart
(Cineteca Bologna)
Recco-Genova
2005

This edition published by
UKA PRESS PUBLISHING
London & Yorkshire, UK
Olympiaweg 102-hs, 1076 XG, Amsterdam, The Netherlands
St. A, 108, Shida, Fujieda, Shizuoka 426-0071, Japan

A CIP catalogue record for this book is available
at the British Library

ISBN : 978-1-906796-24-3
(1-906796-24-6)

Stills in this volume copyright Roy Export Company Establishment, Douris Corporation and Photoplay Productions

This book was prepared for print by UKA Press
and printed in Great Britain

To David Gill, to whose talent and tenacity we
owe these documentaries

and

to David Robinson, on whose knowledge and
helpfulness we were so dependent

Contents

Preface	7
1. The Shock of Discovery	11
2. Buried Treasure	19
3. The Next Battle	26
4. To Switzerland	43
5. Another Think Coming	45
6. 'I Never Give Interviews'	49
7. Whatever Next?	65
8. The Circus	73
9. Luminous Excursions	77
10. Vault Farce	85
11. Evidence of our Eyes	87
12. Light Blue Touchpaper...	99
13. Over There	103
14. Celtic Twilight	111
15. Too Good to Last	131
16. Inching Forward	161
17. If Walls Could Speak	165
18. Rohauer's Story	171
19. Assembling the Material	179
Epilogue	195
Credits	199
Appendix: Watching Chaplin direct (1966)	201
Index	210
Acknowledgements	217

In February 1983, shortly after *Unknown Chaplin* had been shown on television, a Spanish journalist telephoned David Gill and told him he wanted to write about the series.

"I hated Chaplin," he said, with unexpected vehemence, "until I saw your programme. I thought him so Victorian. And ugly. When I saw your prints – so sharp and clear – it was an entirely different experience. Now I change my mind. I think I do article on the Charlie Chaplin revival."

Preface

In the world of film collecting, the claim "find of the century" may sound an unpardonable exaggeration. But what discovery can equal it?[1] Collectors had hailed the discovery of the occasional lost Keystone comedy in which Chaplin played, but nobody had the slightest idea that somewhere in England, somewhere in France, and somewhere in the United States lay three separate treasure troves of silent film which would, for the first time, reveal the working methods of the greatest single figure of the cinema. It was a treasure hunt involving innocence and guile, accident and coincidence. A treasure hunt which took us to Switzerland, France and the United States. The treasure, when it was uncovered, revealed information as precious as the film itself. From the material, we compiled a television series called *Unknown Chaplin*, three hour-long documentaries produced for Thames Television.

Apart from the experience of making the series, we learned so much about Chaplin we could not squeeze into the commentary we decided to preserve it in the form of a book.

When we began research, the first thing that struck us was the paucity of knowledge about Chaplin as a filmmaker. His private life had been splashed across the newspapers of the world, and the vicious melange given the dignity of hard covers. With so much gossip to occupy their attention, journalists could hardly be expected to care how the man made his films, even if those films were the most successful ever made. Yet one expects more from serious historians.

Something like three hundred books have been published about Chaplin. So many follow the same line – a recounting of the life, followed by the stories of the films – you begin to suspect that the authors have read five and written a sixth. Virtually none of them took the trouble to interview Chaplin's associates.

Albert Austin (d.1953), Henry Bergman (d.1946) and Edna Purviance (d.1958) were overlooked, despite the wealth of information they would have been able to provide. And Sydney Chaplin (d.1965),

---

1. I have used it about the miraculous discovery by Wales Film Archive of the 1918 epic on David Lloyd George, which certainly deserved it, despite being ignored shamefully by the press and even by Welsh Channel 4.

Charlie's half-brother, would have known more than any of them, yet only one author, R.J. Minney, bothered to capture any of his memories. I write harshly on the subject, yet I am to blame myself. When I began researching the silent cinema, Sydney as well as Charlie, was still alive. Yet Chaplin was low on my scale of priorities. I was convinced that everything that could be said about him had already been said – repeatedly. By the time I realised how wrong I was, it was too late.

Fortunately, David Robinson published his masterly biography in 1985 – too late for our programme, but not too late for him to play a vital part in getting it to happen.

In our researches, we found that Chaplin's assistant on *The Circus* and *City Lights*, Harry Crocker, had written his memoirs. (The unpublished manuscript is preserved at the Academy library.) And Eddie Sutherland, assistant on *A Woman of Paris* and *The Gold Rush*, had recorded his. (The tape and transcript is at the Oral History Department of Columbia University.) Even more important, someone had persuaded Chaplin to sit down and talk into a tape recorder – and that story is worth relating in the detail it deserves. While some of the information we found is supported by documents, and can thus be proved, a great deal of it comes under the heading of educated guesswork. We worked very much like archaeologists, studying the evidence of our eyes. To be strictly accurate, I should use the phrase "might have" a great deal, for my comments on the Mutuals, for instance, are surmisals only. But they are surmisals based on such strong evidence that it would be irritating to be so half-hearted. I want to make this clear at the start, for the benefit of future historians of Chaplin's work.

Throughout the book, I use the name Chaplin for the man, and Charlie for the character.

In England, where Chaplin was born and where he enjoyed the fan worship usually reserved for royalty, public opinion has undergone a radical change. As though embarrassed by the adulation of their elders, new generations have poured cold water over Chaplin's reputation. Opinions, however, are not facts. The fact that neither Buster Keaton or Harold Lloyd, the two other great silent comedians, could have come to prominence without their way being paved by Chaplin's huge commercial success is beside the point. The fact that Chaplin's early, and admittedly crude, comedies of 1914-15 are compared to Keaton's of the sophisticated 1920s is also irrelevant. The important fact is that Chaplin was, in his time, the phenomenon of the age. No one was so famous, no one better loved. It is impossible for anyone who has not experienced it to understand it. A letter we received from a viewer, Douglas Johnson of Ilford, Essex, conveys a hint of it: 'Whenever a Chaplin film was showing the whole audience was intent on laughing and enjoying every gesture. The feeling throughout the cinema would be electrifying. It was wonderful to be participating in the warmth being shown to Charlie and his supporting players. During my school years, you were either a Chaplin fan or a Harold Lloyd fan, almost dividing the class into two. My father would tell me "Given an empty room as a set, Charlie could by himself make you laugh, whereas Harold would have great difficulty without his props." And that remained my argument for many years.'

The fact that Chaplin's great films are so seldom shown, either in the cinema or on television, is a crippling drawback. Yet, paradoxically, Chaplin is an over-exposed comedian. His earliest, and least impressive work, being long out of copyright, is churned out on television in wretched prints with miserable musical accompaniment. As another correspondent, stage producer Peter Cotes, put it, referring to the series: "It was a bonus to have the unadulterated Charlie on the screen, and not in the form that he's been so often; badly re-edited and quite atrociously 'accompanied' by that orchestra so insensitively recorded in the Netherlands sound studio by a barmy band!" Television, of course, is not the medium for which Chaplin's films were designed. Chaplin composed his scenes in loose mid-shots, ideal for the big screen, but not close enough for television. He was also confident of large audiences, united by laughter. A large audience in front of a TV set is five people. The electricity generated in the cinema does not exist. Comedies – and not just Chaplin's comedies – are often watched straight-faced, in stony silence. Laughter is supposed to be infectious; the atmosphere at home is often sterile. This is one reason why TV comedians are supported by canned laughter.

I remember showing some of our discoveries at a film festival. There was a packed audience, and the people roared with laughter. Some were almost hysterical. When we showed those same episodes on videotape on TV monitors, there was no laughter. Oh yes, those watching had enjoyed the sequences, but the experience could hardly have been more different. Let us hope that the great Chaplin films will return to the cinema, where they belong, and that they will be watched by large and appreciative audiences. All it needs is the proper climate. To help create that climate is the purpose of this book.

Kevin Brownlow (1983)

Since 1983, a number of important events have taken place. David Robinson published his masterly biography in 1985 – having helped us immeasurably to get the programme made. His book was republished with new material in 2001. David Shepard brought out excellent prints of the Mutuals on DVD, with Carl Davis scores, through the British Film Institute. MK2 and Warner Bros. have brought out superb transfers of the feature films on DVD. And these features are now being seen in live performance, thanks to composer-conductors Carl Davis and Tim Brock, who tour Europe with 35mm prints.

In 2002, with Michael Kloft of Spiegel Television, I directed a film about the making of the *Great Dictator, The Tramp and the Dictator,* which used colour footage shot on the set by Chaplin's brother Sydney, found in the vaults by Chaplin's children Christopher and Victoria.

Cineteca Bologna has become the repository of Chaplin material. Richard Attenborough directed in 1992 a biographical feature film noted for a remarkable, Oscar-nominated performance from Robert Downey Jr. Several more books on Chaplin have been published and in England, Bristol Silents' 'Slapstick' Festival has attracted – and undeniably converted – large audiences for silent films with orchestra, and for Chaplin in particular.

Thanks to all these efforts, Chaplin's reputation has been returned to something like its original supremacy.

KB (2010)

1. The Shock of Discovery

In September, 1977, David Gill and I were involved in producing *Hollywood*, a series about the American silent film, for Thames Television. Our base was at Teddington studios, just outside London. Since this was over an hour's journey from my home in Belsize Park, David sometimes took pity on me and drove to my place to work on the scripts. "Scripts" is too grand a description for what we produced. "Cutting order" describes them better; we compiled them to give our editors some idea of what to put together.

    This particular morning, neither of us was in a mood to write. David was not long back from holiday, and he had arrived late. He was always late, unless it was really important, when he was even later. But always with excellent reason. However, one was so glad to see him, one always forgave him. In his late forties, he had been with commercial television since its inception in 1955. A greater contrast to the stereotyped image of the TV director, however, would be hard to imagine. His background was ballet – he had been a dancer himself; his wife, Pauline, taught at the Royal Ballet School; and one of his daughters, Judith, was a dancer. His ability to perform dance steps enlivened his stories. He could leave people helpless with laughter, and I often thought that his skill as a physical comedian manqué proved of value again and again during the making of the Chaplin series.

    But you would hardly connect him with ballet, either, at first sight. His half-moon glasses and broad forehead gave him the comforting look of a doctor, which is what his father had been. (His uncle was Eric Gill, among the greatest of British artists.) His mind, however, was that of a barrister. If you engaged his interest, he gave you his complete attention, and woe betide you if you lacked the facts. He would adopt the role of devil's advocate, and dissect your narrative, as though only after the most intense spotlight had been directed on it could he believe it. And no one could interrupt him until he had finished. He had an astonishing capacity for concentration and his relentless thoroughness was one of his prime virtues, although, with unimportant subjects, it could be a hindrance. But it had sustained him through several years of directing the investigative programme *This Week*, and it would sustain us through our most difficult stages.

I had come from a different world – the world of independent film-making, where money was spent with the greatest reluctance, and everyone worked for nothing. I had no idea about expenditure in television. David was not only a director; he was a skilful producer, and it was soon apparent that he was going to occupy the driving seat on the *Hollywood* series.

He did so with such tact and consideration – and such outstanding results – that it maddened me when certain papers gave me sole credit for its success. But he needed a long runway to launch an important project. For the first few weeks, we did nothing but view silent films. It was like being back at school again. For both of us had become interested in films through watching them at boarding school. In David's case, he was given the job of choosing records to accompany the silent films – one of the most useful skills he could possibly have learned as far as the series was concerned. This particular morning, we had to face the numbing task of writing the episode on comedy. Of all thirteen, this was probably the most difficult, simply because there was so much of it. Hundreds of books had been written on the subject, thousands of articles – and an amazing proportion of the films had survived. How do you compress the silent era's richest output into fifty-two minutes?

Comedy, of course, meant Chaplin. We could easily have devoted an episode to Chaplin, but we had been told that the rights to all his copyrighted films had been tied up. ("Copyright", in this case, means post-1917, when Chaplin became independent and started making his finest pictures.) The earlier comedies, made for companies like Keystone, Essanay and Mutual, were out of copyright, but you'd be lucky to find a decent print. Most had been copied and recopied until they were a strain to watch. The distribution of all copyright films was controlled by a company called Black Inc., which had licensed the TV rights in the UK exclusively to the BBC, our rivals. The head of Black Inc. was Mo Rothman, one of the toughest entrepreneurs in the business. Mo Rothman made it quite plain that there was no hope. The BBC had the UK rights until 1988. Complicated licensing arrangements had been made with each country and Black Inc. would not consider untangling them, nor would they permit us to do so.

So we were faced with the absurd situation of having to illustrate Chaplin's work with the films he made before 1917. We knew one person who might be able to help us over this impasse: David Robinson, film critic of the *Times*, was also a Chaplin devotee and had spent many years researching his career in the music halls.[2] When *A Woman of Paris* was reissued, Robinson wrote a review into which he drew all sorts of obscure references to Chaplin's theatrical origins, and as a result he received a Christmas card from the great man. This eventually led to a meeting.[3] David Robinson told us that the Power Behind the Throne was a lady called Rachel Ford, who occupied the role of business manager, although her responsibilities were much wider. He suggested we write to her and David and I composed as heartfelt a plea as we could. No reply. We sent a reminder. We got no reply to that for a long time, and then came a letter confirming that what Black Inc. had told us was unfortunately correct. This, from Miss Ford's secretary, Mme Arène, was followed a few days later by one from Miss Ford herself:

> "I have obtained Sir Charles and Lady Chaplin's permission to produce some little snippet for you. For reasons too complicated to explain, I would want our distributor, Mr Rothman, to know of our desire to help you. I wrote to him last June, but recently learned that as a result of some slight accident which occurred end July he all but died. I understand he has made a complete recovery and is convalescing in California. I have again written to his office with your request. In any case, nothing can be done until I get myself to London, maybe during September. By then I hope to have had some favourable reaction from Rothman, and be able to show you what I have in mind."

September had arrived and we had heard nothing more. We sat down and began to struggle with the mass of material. We wrote an outline for the Mack Sennett sequence, but the logical end to Sennett was the start of Chaplin. "It's hopeless to go on like this," said David, throwing down his pen. "We'll have to try and speak to Miss Ford." He dialled her Paris

2. He has since written the definitive biography of Chaplin.
3. David Robinson attended the music recording sessions of *A Woman of Paris* and was able to talk to Chaplin. He also intervened on our behalf in many different ways with Rachel Ford and Oona Chaplin, and we owe him an enormous debt.

office direct, and was told she was already in England. He had no sooner replaced the receiver, than the phone rang. It was our researcher; Miss Ford had been trying to call us, at our Teddington office, at the precise moment we had been calling her.

David relayed the instructions: call Denham Laboratories, ask for the vaults, and then ask for her. "So that's where the Chaplin vaults are," I told myself as I dialled the number. "And I always thought they were in Switzerland." Once through to the vaults, I heard a beautifully modulated, upper-class English voice which managed to infuse a great deal of suspicion into the simple word "Hello?" I explained who I was, and Miss Ford announced: "I have a little snippet for you. It may be no use at all. Could you come here this day and see it? Or perhaps send someone to pick it up?" "We will come at once," I said. I checked my watch, and saw that it was midday. "Perhaps we could take you out to lunch?" "No," she said. "There is a little pub we always go to for lunch. It gets a little crowded and we like to get there just before one. Denham is about an hour's drive from London. Come down as fast as you can. But don't break the speed limit."

David drove down to Denham in a mere forty minutes, parked at the labs, next to the historic old Korda studios; a lab technician guided us to the vaults. We entered a hangar-like shed packed to the roof with old film cans, with titles like *Lady Hamilton, Above us the Waves*, and new ones, with titles like *Valentino, Jesus, Genesis*... Filtering through these fascinating corridors of cans, we emerged into a brightly-lit passageway where we met Miss Ford.

Miss Ford was in her sixties, I judged (she later told us she was seventy-four). She was trim and neat, protecting her sensible clothes with a dust-jacket and white gloves. At first sight, she was somewhat formidable, despite her slight build; one sensed she was accustomed to being obeyed. The vault was as neat as she was. I was a trifle disappointed at the sight of rows of gleaming cans, the famous titles stencilled on sheets of typing paper proclaiming one pile to be THE GOLD RUSH, another CITY LIGHTS and another THE GREAT DICTATOR. I had hoped for jumbles of rusty tins, cobwebbed corners and some fascinating surprises.

Miss Ford explained that she was now working for us, looking for a short sequence we could use for our "snippet". David and I exchanged doleful glances. A snippet would scarcely sustain a fifty-two minute programme; even if we reduced the Chaplin section to half an episode, we still needed a sequence from *The Kid*. We had interviewed Jackie Coogan in Palm Springs, California, and he had spoken movingly of his experience with Chaplin on that picture. Without it, we were lost. And Miss Ford made it clear that *The Kid* was within Mo Rothman's domain – she was in search of material that lay outside it.

"I have found a can from *The Circus*," she said mysteriously, as we travelled to a second vault. "And now we're looking for a can from *Modern Times*. But I should have realised – you are only concerned with the silent film era." We explained that since Chaplin had extended the silent era by making silents well into the 1930s, it would be marvellous if we could acknowledge that fact in the series.

We entered the second vault. The same system, the stencilled labels, the gleaming cans. But suddenly my eyes fell on an unfamiliar title. "What was *The Professor*?" I asked. "Oh, that was a fun film," she said dismissively. "You can have that, but it isn't funny. It was made in the studio, just for fun, and I saw it and it isn't very good. I asked Charlie about it and he said 'Oh, that means nothing'."

Both David and I were stunned. "You mean there are films here that were never released?" "Oh, yes," said Miss Ford, as if it were the most natural thing in the world. She managed to find a partial list of the contents of these cans: one batch was called *Visitors to the Studio*. We noticed it included General Wood, Maxine Elliott, Max Linder and Jackie Coogan! Miss Ford must have read our expressions, even though we tried to remain cool, calm and poker-faced. "First, lunch," she said.

In the Land of Liberty pub, Miss Ford recalled coming to Denham Studios in the 1930s, when they were owned by Alexander Korda,[4] and watching Charles Laughton at work. It was her only visit to a studio. She was more interested in the theatre and music than in the cinema. We gathered that during the war, Rachel Ford had been an officer in the French Army Medical Corps. She sounded so English we were puzzled by the French connection. "My father was half Irish and half French, and he married a French woman, who died when I was six, so I'm three-quarters French. But I came to a London school in the First World

---

4. She said the film he was making was *The Private Life of Henry VIII* which was not made at Denham.

War and lost my French and had to start all over again afterwards. My father always maintained I spoke no known language."

She was head of a French (Red Cross) Army Medical Service near Metz at the Fall of France. "I had the fantastic good fortune to run into my father in Bordeaux – we reached London quickly and I found General De Gaulle's Free French forces." She went on the Dakar Expedition and served in the Free French Medical Service in London-Normandy, ending up head of 2,000 French ATS (AFAT: Auxiliaires Féminins de l'Armée de Terre), attaining the highest rank possible for a woman in the French Army. She was awarded the Croix de Guerre in 1940 with "palme" and the Legion d'Honneur in 1944. She worked for five years in the European Movement, organising conferences, before being introduced to Chaplin.

The Chaplins were in Switzerland for a house-hunting expedition. They moved into the Manoir de Ban at Vevey in early January, 1953, just before lunch and Rachel arrived at 2 pm. "I was a terrific fan, and I only went to see him because I wanted to meet him, not because of the job. I told him I couldn't be a secretary because I couldn't spell and couldn't type and was hopeless with figures. I was wearing one man's ski boot and one woman's shoe, having suffered a burn, and I had lost my dog's lead. I kept saying 'I couldn't help you... I'd be no use at all. I know nothing about films'." Chaplin hired her but said: "I must warn you, you'll be mixing with the scum of the earth."

Referring to the "fun films," she said that Chaplin had told her to burn them. "He didn't say that because he didn't want anyone to see them. He honestly felt that no one would be interested in seeing them. He is a genuinely modest man." Chaplin had jokingly signed a paper assigning them to Miss Ford. I seized the opportunity of asking the question all film historians argue about: did Chaplin destroy the negative of the film von Sternberg made for him, *The Sea Gull*?[5] "I am convinced it was burned. I not only look after the films – and there is no sign of it in the vaults – I also look after his private papers. I am sure I would have come across a reference to it somewhere, but there is nothing."

---

5. When researching the private papers of Sydney Chaplin at Vevey, David Robinson discovered a document, signed and witnessed, proving that the negative of *The Sea Gull* had been destroyed in the '30s.

On the way back to the vaults, Miss Ford declared that the one type of person she couldn't abide was the film collector. (This made me blanch, for I was a film collector.) Evidently, she was constantly suing them. "Charlie is very reasonable about most things," she laughed, "but whenever he hears about someone pirating his films, he says 'Put them in prison. They're my films, and that's that'." She added that *The Kid* was the one film she found most difficulty in rounding up, and suspected that it must have been duped (copied) before it was released. "I cannot tell you how much has been spent suing pirates," she said, and she told us about the longest court case, against a collector and distributor called Raymond Rohauer. He had discovered that when Chaplin reissued *The Gold Rush* with narration and music in 1942, this constituted a new version. Chaplin had a staff to take care of this sort of thing. Apparently, the person who looked after such matters thought that reissuing a film automatically protected the original copyright. When he realised the copyright on the 1925 version had lapsed, Rohauer decided to distribute it himself. The lawsuit against Rohauer dragged on for twelve years, consuming thousands of dollars. He had become Miss Ford's *bête noire*.

The curious thing about Rohauer was the antipathy he had aroused. I, too, was one of his sworn opponents. I objected to the way he bought up vast tracts of the silent cinema, secured some kind of rights over them, and denied anyone access except at vast cost. He had formed a partnership with Douglas Fairbanks Jr. to control the Fairbanks Senior films, and forced film appreciation societies, like the British Film Institute and the Museum of Modern Art, to withdraw all their Fairbanks films from circulation. He followed this with the Keaton, Langdon and Sennett films. I had helped John Baxter research an article about him in the *Sunday Times*. (Rohauer sued, won and settled out of court for an undisclosed sum.)

If there was one thing I was determined to prevent on the *Hollywood* series it was any sort of contact with Raymond Rohauer. And I had succeeded for the first few months, until we ran into the problem of the Fairbanks films. We had an excellent interview with Douglas Fairbanks Jr., and we needed first-class quality extracts from his father's films. "All you have to do," he had told us, "is talk to Raymond Rohauer. He'll give you anything you want." I gave up.

Our executive producer, Mike Wooller, made the initial approaches; David Gill had taken over. Not having the backlog of distrust, and not being a collector, he was able to meet Rohauer as a normal human being. He was relieved, he told us, not to encounter an ogre. David greeted him warmly with "It's a pleasure to meet you," and he could see the surprise in his eyes. He formed a relationship which produced a great deal of rare footage for the series. But this was not the time to acquaint Rachel Ford with such facts. Another of Miss Ford's *bêtes noires* was Mo Rothman – "the bandit", as she called him with admirable bluntness. The two of them were constantly involved in quarrels, and for this reason she was anxious not to trespass on his domain. And she was quick to pay tribute where it was due: "Mo did a marvellous job with the special shows," she said. "They couldn't have been better done. The Piazza San Marco in Venice was black with people. He brought a special projector from Sweden and showed *City Lights* on a huge screen – it was magnificent. I mean to say, the man's a crook, but I would never say that I regretted him having the films. Charlie had terrific pleasure out of them at the end of his life, and what's $200,000 more or less to him? It wouldn't make much difference. Roy Export – Charlie's company – owns it, but Mo has the licence. And it would be very difficult for me, since he has sold the rights to the BBC, to ask him. Whereas there is no question that Roy owns the private material, and we can give you a snippet from that. You don't want much, after all, do you? A minute should do..." David and I made anxious noises. "Well, perhaps two minutes. Anyway, the snippet I have in mind is one of my favourite moments. Absolutely delightful. He does a little dance. But I'm not quite sure where it is..." We returned to the vaults, and Miss Ford selected four cans. We carried them to the projection room (suppressing a desire to run for the street), exhilarated by the extraordinary personality we had just met, and by the prospect of what was before us.

2. Buried Treasure

We settled into the plush projection theatre with a mixture of excitement and anxiety. Whatever we found among these rolls, we would not have a programme without *The Kid*. The first can was marked, cryptically, CL/MT TRAFFIC SEQUENCE. Miss Ford explained that it was a sequence cut before release from either *Modern Times* or *City Lights*, no one was sure As soon as it appeared on the screen, we saw that it had been shot with sound masking, the smaller frame area which appeared after the introduction of sound, which meant that it had to be post-*City Lights*. It was mute – without sound – and, like everything else we saw, of surpassingly good quality.

In the days before traffic lights, automatic signs resembling railway signals were used in American cities – moving arms marked STOP and GO. The sequence began with a closeup of one of these, and then a long shot showed Charlie approaching the busy intersection. He thinks the GO sign refers to him, and blithely crosses the street. Several cars screech to a halt. He makes the other side safely, but a cop orders him back. Charlie gestures that he doesn't want to – he's going the opposite way. The cop, irritated by his seeming idiocy, grabs him and forces him to the other sidewalk. Buffeted by other pedestrians, Charlie dutifully waits for the GO sign and sets off again. The cop is livid. Forcing cars to a halt, he manhandles Charlie back across the street, points to the sign and insists he start again. The signal changes. The cop says he should now cross. No thanks, gestures Charlie. He thinks he'll stay this side after all...

The sequence obviously belonged in *Modern Times*, where Charlie is caught in the machine age, a victim of assembly-line automation. The sequence was cut, presumably, because while it was amusing, there were no strong gags in it. It was well-staged, but slight. The next sequence was anything but. Quite clearly from *City Lights*, it was also quite clearly the original opening. The statue, which is unveiled in the opening of the film as we know it, is still covered in the establishing long shot. Cut to a shop window on a street corner. Through the glass, we see Charlie shambling along the busy sidewalk. He pauses in front of the shop window, eyeing the passing girls with a faintly wicked look. A piece of wood, stuck in a sidewalk grille, just beneath the window, attracts his attention. He pokes at it with his cane. The stick revolves in its trap, but it will not drop. Charlie becomes obsessive, striking at it more and more energetically. A passer-by pauses to watch. In a moment, a crowd has gathered. Charlie looks around, startled, and, embarrassed at the fuss he has caused, raises his hat. The crowd disappears.

A delivery boy ambles up and stares at him. He is wearing uniform, but his dopey expression belies the EXPRESS on his cap.[6] Charlie adopts an expression of world-weary superiority. The boy is eating an orange, and spits out the pips. Charlie gets juice in the eye, so to avoid this fellow, he walks to the other side of the shop window and watches him balefully through the glass. When the Express boy makes his own attempts to jab at the piece of wood, Charlie returns, protectively, only to get a direct hit in the eye again... The boy wanders off and two women step up to the window to examine the clothes. One straddles the piece of wood. Very slowly and carefully, Charlie eases forward but, as his foot makes contact with the wood, it also makes contact with the woman's leg. She turns, glowers at him with horror and loathing and walks around the corner with her friend. A man – a window-dresser (Harry Crocker) – appears in the window and spots what Charlie is doing. He gives him advice. Charlie mimes that he cannot hear. The window-dresser turns back to his work, but he is profoundly irritated by Charlie's futile efforts. He too wants to free the stick. (The power of this little piece of wood seems to overwhelm all other concerns.) He remonstrates with his ruler. Charlie cannot hear. The man yells at full volume and the floor-walkers pop into the window, wondering what all the noise is about. By now a crowd has gathered again. The window-dresser becomes so annoyed by Charlie's stupidity that he fails to notice a mannequin has been replaced by a salesgirl, and he jams a pricetag and pin into her rear. She shrieks and runs off. A policeman fights his way through the crowd, which now stretches across the street, and Charlie, in a moment of expertise brought on by panic, manages to dislodge the wood. He raises his hat and exits, and the policeman disperses the crowd.

This sequence was a revelation. David looked at me in amazement. "Have you ever seen that before?" "Never." David later confessed that

---

6. David Robinson discovered that this part was played by Charles Lederer, Marion Davies' nephew, screenwriter of *His Girl Friday*.

he was absolutely sick with excitement, realising that we were seeing a film which Chaplin had shot and cut, and of which he had made a graded print – absolutely complete and perfect, in its own way – and which had lain on the shelf unknown to anyone outside Chaplin's immediate circle for fifty years. It was pure cinema – no subtitles were needed, no sound effects could have improved it. The sequence was the essence of Chaplin's art. For he, more than anyone else in pictures, could take the smallest object, the least promising prop, and turn it into a fabulously funny sequence.

Miss Ford sensed our emotion. "I thought it would amuse you," she smiled, "but you can't have it." The excitement of discovery was tempered by reality. We felt remarkably privileged and extremely deprived at the same moment.

Visitors Reel 1A followed. The first item must have been filmed in 1917 or 1918 since most of the men are in uniform. The notes in the can refer to "General Wood". Chaplin, in civilian clothes, is showing the General around the studio. The General asks to see the tramp outfit. Chaplin takes him to a dressing table, and produces the famous boots and baggy trousers He holds the trousers up to show how enormous they are, and then smears his upper lip with spirit gum and puts on the moustache. This we could use; Jackie Coogan told us that he always knew when it was time to go to work, for he smelt spirit gum. I had no idea who the General was but I discovered later that Leonard Wood had been a cavalry officer in the frontier days, who had fought Geronimo and the Apache. A close friend of Theodore Roosevelt, he had become army Chief of Staff, but was passed over for supreme command when America entered the war and instead took command of home defence. In 1919, during the Red Scare, he noted with approval a minister's call for the deportation of Bolshevists "in ships of stone with sails of lead, with the wrath of God for a breeze and with hell for their first port". Chaplin's political troubles had not yet begun, of course, otherwise General Wood would not have been so keen to visit his studio.

Also in uniform was the next visitor, marked on the can simply as "Bishop".[7] The date was not given on the notes, but it also had to be 1918-1919 since the scene takes place on an exterior set for *Sunnyside*, which was released in July 1919. Chaplin is in tramp costume and he

---

7. The Bishop of Birmingham.

demonstrates his walk, and his trick with his hat and cane. In the background appears Sydney, Charlie's older brother, wheeling a penny farthing bicycle. Charlie scrambles aboard, and promptly falls off. Sydney demonstrates it with cool aplomb, riding around the set until he becomes over-confident, hits too high a speed, and falls off himself.

A delightful surprise followed. Chaplin was shown relaxing in an armchair when through the French windows appears Max Linder. David and I gasped aloud at this, because in our tentative script for the comedy episode, Max Linder played an important role. He had been the first international star of comedy films. Starting his career in 1905, and working for Pathé Frères, Linder had created a characterisation of a well-to-do buffoon, usually wearing a silk hat, whose closest relative in films was to be Adolphe Menjou. But he influenced Chaplin, and, at least at this period, Chaplin acknowledged the debt. He signed a photograph "To the Professor from his pupil". Linder and Chaplin embrace, and we next see them on the sidewalk, in front of a large limousine. Linder imitates Charlie's walk then Chaplin, not to be outdone, begins a splendidly exaggerated version of Max Linder, going on his knees and kissing Linder's hand. At first, Linder doesn't quite understand, and when he does, he looks uncomfortable, as if to say "Come on, you are going too far!" Before we had time to recover, up came the sequence with Jackie Coogan. In front of a large, and unfortunately anonymous, group of visitors,[8] Jackie Coogan does an act, with Charlie as straight man. He falls over in a dead faint, and Charlie scoops him up by the neck with the handle of his cane. Then he does the shimmy until, grinning broadly, Charlie pretends to kick him out of shot. After a moment, Jackie runs back in and takes up his position for applause. "This must be the sequence you were thinking of," we said. "The dance?" "No, it's not," said Miss Ford, "but yes, you can have that. It's not Mo's."

Among a group of visitors by the studio gates is actress Maxine Elliott. A celebrated stage actress, Miss Elliott was, in 1919, being starred in pictures by Chaplin's friend Sam Goldwyn. In ordinary clothes, Chaplin obliges with a demonstration of his walk, to the evident delight of the group. Inside, on a set for *Sunnyside* of the hotel lobby, they stage a little scene. Maxine, as a prospective guest, arrives

---

8. Glenn Mitchell identifies them as First National exhibitors.

Rollie Totheroh on *The Floorwalker* (1916), Chaplin's first for Mutual

at the front desk and bangs on the bell. Charlie appears, in full costume. She signs in and Charlie twiddles the pen on the back of her hand. He leads her down the corridor to her room and, giving her a very naughty look, suggests she should follow. She does, but there's something amiss. Charlie rushes back to his cubby-hole and emerges with a tiny tin bath. Maxine Elliott breaks up. End of scene.

The *Sunnyside* hotel set came in useful for another famous visitor, Crown Prince Axel of Denmark. He, too, wants to see Charlie's walk. Chaplin obliges with a demonstration, but he twirls his cane too energetically and knocks his hat off. He suggests they make a film, co-starring Edna Purviance. In one shot, we see Chaplin organising the royal entourage. In the next, the Crown Prince, incredibly tall, blond and Scandinavian, arrives at the lobby with an armful of suitcases. Charlie tries, unsuccessfully, to persuade him to stay. He is just about to leave when Edna passes majestically down the corridor. Axel drops the suitcases, signs in, and vanishes down the corridor in search of Edna, with Charlie galloping after him with all the cases.

The final visitor on the reel was filmed in a bedroom set for *Sunnyside*. (Chaplin wrote in his autobiography that he was having marital problems with his first wife, Mildred Harris, and making *Sunnyside* was like "pulling teeth". No doubt he regarded these visitors as welcome diversions.) Author Irvin Cobb, who wrote novels of homespun humour, digs into his pocket and produces a huge bundle of bills. Charlie rushes in and out, doing his bidding, and all he gets is a handshake. He produces the little tin bath and suggests Cobb puts his tip in there. The tip is so tiny, he takes back his bath.

The screening ended with two reels from *The Circus*, which Miss Ford was anxious we should see, because she thought they might contain the dance. We were startled to see a slate board at the front, and to realise we were watching not just cut sequences but uncut rushes.

In the silent days, just as today, every shot was given a separate number. Not with a clapper board – the clapper was only useful for synchronising action and sound for talking pictures – but with an ordinary slate board. The usual method was for the scene number to be chalked up with the take number – thus Scene 200, if taken three times, would be 200-3. Chaplin avoided this method, and settled for one overall number, which changed with every take. Thus this roll of rushes began with slate 3658. We soon realised why he preferred this method; it disguised the large number of takes.

Most of this roll took place in a restaurant. Charlie has taken Merna Kennedy, the girl, to dinner, and somehow his rival, Harry Crocker, has come too. Charlie falls foul of a prizefighter, who delights in taunting him by flicking sugar lumps at his hat. The shots were taken out of order, and suddenly a board would appear – 3722 – and Charlie would emerge from his caravan in a totally different location. One sequence, filmed in master shot, was hilarious: on the sidewalk a lady has dropped a parcel full of fish. Charlie offers to pick it up, but as soon as he does so, the fish fall out. He raises his hat and takes hurried leave of a hopeless cause, but the woman calls him back and insists on his help. He wraps up the parcel, but the slithery fish keep slipping out. Maddened, she grabs the paper, places it across his arms, and, kneeling on the ground, loads him up. He manages to drop a couple on her head.

Suddenly, his legs begin to writhe, and pushing the parcel into her hands, he produces a fish from inside his trousers. He raises his hat and leaves abruptly, to the woman's fury.

This scene was repeated again and again. Because it was shot on a Hollywood street – very unusual for Chaplin and perhaps caused by a recent fire at his studio – curious bystanders tend to wander into shot. And people pass from shop to shop in the background. Onlookers are reflected in shop windows. Chaplin relentlessly continues, with an apparently unlimited supply of fish, day after day. At one moment, the actress loses her composure, sniffs her hands in disgust and (apparently) gives vent to a stream of complaints. But the camera stops before one can be sure. What one can be sure of is that any humour the scene contained is well and truly ground under by constant repetition. Seeing all these shots together made us wonder how anyone could think them funny – or anything funny – once they've been exposed to take after take after take. It says a great deal for Chaplin's judgement that he could sustain his critical eye over the months, even years, his films took to make. Then Charlie does his wild squiggle before producing the fish from his trousers and we're laughing again. Miss Ford was disappointed that the scene she wanted – the little dance – was not on these rolls. But we weren't. For we knew it meant we'd have to return and look at some more.

But still we were no nearer *The Kid*. Miss Ford could not understand why we were so insistent. "If you see the Coogan interview, you'll understand," we told her. She agreed to see it, next time she was in London. On the drive back, David and I mulled over the extraordinary glimpses into what Chaplin regarded as his second-best. "That *City Lights* sequence," said David, "was like a perfect, self-contained short story by Chekhov." We didn't say anything to each other at the time, but we both registered the same thought. One day, we had to find a way of using all this material...

3. The Next Battle

Having once glimpsed forbidden fruit, it was hard to resume life as though it didn't exist. Our script for the comedy episode became more ambitious, and incorporated some of this material. While we had no permission to use it, we had unlimited hope. The fly in the ointment was Mo Rothman. The *Hollywood* series was based on interviews, and its whole impact would depend on our bringing together word and picture. The "I was there" approach would fall very flat if we had to resort to stills, or an irrelevant scene. Jackie Coogan had given us a memorable and moving interview which could not possibly work without the film he described. Whether or not we won permission to use the private material, as we had learned to call it, we were far more desperate for permission to use *The Kid*. We had to win Rachel Ford to our cause, and two months after our first meeting, she returned to London. I met her at the Savoy, and in a hired car, we drove to Teddington. *En route*, she talked of a journalist (Frederick Sands) who had recently won fame with an interview with Garbo for *Bunte Illustrierte*. It wasn't much of an interview – more a few words over a cup of coffee – but Sands had hidden a cameraman and secured pictures of himself with Garbo. Miss Ford recalled that Sands had had himself photographed arriving at the Chaplin house in Switzerland. "Unfortunately," she said, "he didn't get in." So he wrote an article culled from Charlie's autobiography, dealing largely with the paternity suit. "The following week, there was a letter from a reader objecting to the tone of the piece and saying that, since Chaplin had given the world so much pleasure, perhaps it would be best to let sleeping dogs lie. The editor disagreed: Sands was 'an intimate friend' of Chaplin's and as such his testimony was of public interest. This infuriated Oona, who sent a telegram they were obliged to print."

At Teddington, Miss Ford was introduced to the other members of the Hollywood team, and she proceeded to captivate everybody. David and I escorted her to the theatre, where we screened for her the Jackie Coogan interview. This was a crucial test. If she approved of it, she would intercede on our behalf with Mo Rothman. If not... but we had no qualms. We had filmed it a few months earlier in Palm Springs. And Coogan had not lost his admiration for Chaplin. It became apparent that his year on *The Kid* was the highpoint of his life. David had been greatly impressed by *The Kid*, and he wanted to stress the quality of the relationship between Coogan and Chaplin. Jackie Coogan must have told the story a thousand times, and at first he repeated what he'd always said. But in between each roll, David urged me to ask supplementary questions, and he talked to Coogan himself. Coogan, realising he had someone genuinely interested, opened up, and his recollections became fresh and vivid and charged with emotion. It is hard enough to capture such emotion on film; it is impossible in cold type. But here are extracts from the interview we showed Miss Ford:

"Chaplin – he is really unfathomable. You can't pin him down. His talent was so great, so varied. He could do anything, and if he didn't know how to do something, he wouldn't say that he didn't know how, but don't show up the next day, because he could tell you everything about it, or do it better than the guy that originated it. This man was a great tumbler. He had great control of his body. Strong, immensely strong, he had the ability to do anything with his feet or hands or head or torso. If you said 'What?' when you were watching Chaplin, you were lost. All you could do was just watch him – and try to catch him. He had nothing goading him on. He was his own boss and he took the most precious thing in the world – time – and lavished it on the picture. As everyone knows, Charlie wore a crepe moustache and he used to stick it on with spirit gum. And we had several close scenes and this glue had sort of an offensive odour. A lot of the time we were sitting around without an idea, and suddenly he'd get this idea and he'd disappear and get his makeup on. It was fresh and that odour would come through from that glue and that was always associated with 'Well, it's time to go to work'.

[In *The Kid*, the small boy has been looked after by the tramp since he was a baby. Suddenly the Welfare Authorities try to take him away.] And they take him by force, which was practically condemning a child to death. And I can remember him explaining to me what he wanted me to do. Then he also explained why he wanted me to do that. He said, 'Because, Jackie, it's this little boy; he's being torn from his friend.' And as he started to dramatize it, I saw it in my mind's eye. He was a marvellous story-teller, narrator. And he put it on an intensely personal basis, so that when he said 'Camera' and then 'Action', and the Welfare Worker threw me into this truck, that's when the dam broke. Of course, I was really gone. I was torn up: 'I want my daddy', and I was hysterical. And if you are going to portray yourself as being hysterical, you better get yourself hysterical or, brother, it's as phoney as a three-dollar bill."

Rachel Ford did not say a great deal, but what she did say reassured us. "He is very good, isn't he?" We also showed her a film called *Nice and Friendly*. Chaplin made this as a wedding present for Lord Louis Mountbatten in 1921. It featured the Mountbattens and their entourage and Jackie Coogan, and it was shot at Pickfair. "It was just a gag," said Coogan, "a memento. Who would ever have thought that the people involved in it would some day mean as much to other people as those people did? It was a travesty within a travesty of the old English play. Butlers, menacing hands from behind the hedge. My father was in charge of all strangulation on that picture. He had very expressive hands and they were used to threaten people as they came through bushes or doors."

We had obtained *Nice and Friendly* from Lord Mountbatten himself. He had even agreed to an interview, and we showed that to Miss Ford, too. We felt that, having been in the war herself, and having worked for Churchill and De Gaulle, she could hardly fail to be impressed by our coup. We had filmed Mountbatten at his London apartment, and I recall how warmly he had talked of the cinema. He had been responsible for installing projectors in naval vessels. He demonstrated his uncanny knack of remembering people by recognising the sound man who had been on the Mountbatten television series. I was surprised to find not an aloof military man but an amusing character who reminded me of the veteran actor Wilfred Hyde-White. He sat in his mews flat, surrounded by original portraits by Romney, and talked of Chaplin with cheerful affection.

"He was an extraordinary chap – a delightful sense of humour. He was very parsimonious and careful with his money except when he got artistic. He'd engage a complete orchestra to come down and play and then would suddenly become terribly interested in conducting them, so he spent hundreds of dollars just conducting them, which was not part of the film, while the rest of us just watched him. Then he suggested he'd like to give us a wedding present, a film, and with pencil and paper he scribbled an outline of the plot, which was to take in most of my party, including my valet. He spent three days at it. What was rather fun and what amused his own team very much was that it was the first time he had appeared in his ordinary clothes.[9] He directed the whole idea. He taught my wife very quickly – she was very good. He tried to teach me, and then, of course, was very uncomplimentary about my acting. There was a picture taken of him with his hand on my shoulder. He said 'look depressed', so I put my head down and he published it in his book 'Breaking the news to Lord Mountbatten that he is no actor'. The day the film was to start, at two o'clock in the morning, he sent a Hawaiian guitar party to serenade us in the morning to get us in the right mood before the film started. Really, it is impossible to describe the effect that Charlie Chaplin had. He was not only a genius of the silent film, but he produced a new dimension of human slapstick, always extremely intelligent and amusing. And with pathos, too.

"We managed to keep out the press to a remarkable degree in Hollywood. They were very kind and they understood we were on our honeymoon and they weren't allowed in. But the payoff was that we had to arrange to see them once. They took a photograph of my wife guiding the lawn mower and Charlie and me pulling it on ropes. This photograph was sent all over the world and met with strong disapproval from His Majesty King George V. When we came back, he said 'I saw a photograph of you manicuring Charlie Chaplin's lawn. I don't think that was very digni-

---

9. Not quite. He appeared out of make-up and in his street clothes in *Tango Tangles* (1914).

Lord Mountbatten (r) and Chaplin on the lawn at Pickfair during the production of *Nice and Friendly* (1921)

fied, was it?' And not long before he died, a matter, therefore, of some thirteen years later, I went to say goodbye before I went out to take command of the *Daring*. 'By the way,' he said, 'did I ever tell you I didn't approve of your publicity with Douglas Fairbanks and Mary Pickford?' I said, 'Sir, over the years, it has gradually dawned on me you didn't like it'."

Miss Ford was impressed by the interviews, and she asked for them put on cassette for Chaplin. Just for fun we showed her part of a Billy West film. Billy West's speciality was to make himself up to look exactly like Chaplin. The Eric Campbell figure in his comedies was played by a young actor named Oliver Hardy. Miss Ford was dismissive, and felt Billy West had very little talent.

After lunch, as we walked back to the office, she told me that she was worried about Mo Rothman. "What about the private material?" I asked. "Oh, that's unrestricted," she said. I was elated, misunderstanding her terminology. I thought she meant that we would have unrestricted access to it. Only much later did I realise that she was referring to the fact that it was not licensed to Rothman. This misunderstanding caused complications later on.

The following month, on Christmas Day 1977, Charlie Chaplin died. This sad event was followed by a sick one, when the body was dug up and held for ransom by a couple of crazy East European expatriates. The anxiety increased when threats were made against the children. Not surprisingly, we did not see Miss Ford for some time. It was towards the end of March, 1978, when Rachel Ford asked us to come to see her at the Savoy. We raced up from Teddington to find her tired and preoccupied. She had not had a day off since the death and the bodysnatch. Instead of a relaxed meal at Rule's, we had a cramped meeting in her hotel room. We talked of the "snippets" and she said she had Oona's permission to allow us the scenes with Coogan, Max Linder, and General Wood. I now realise how generous she was being, and I am acutely embarrassed when I remember my next remark. David told me later that he was hoping against hope that I wouldn't bring it up. "What about *City Lights*?" I asked. Miss Ford's patience snapped. "I was considering asking Oona's permission to let you have it, but I feel it is ill-advised," she said, firmly and distinctly. "If you don't think you have enough, then we'll just forget the whole thing."

We extricated ourselves as best we could, and consoled ourselves downstairs with a pot of Savoy tea. Miss Ford said she had supported our case to Mo Rothman, but we were still far from securing the rights to *The Kid*. As if to add salt to our wounds, *The Kid* was shown at the NFT in a tribute to Chaplin the following month. David and I went to a press show. I had seen a poor-quality print a few years earlier, and had not been impressed. Here was a beautifully graded, crisp print with Chaplin's own score. I was absolutely stunned by the emotional impact. Even without a proper audience – there were less than half a dozen people there – the picture worked superbly. It immediately became my favourite Chaplin picture. David, who had conducted a campaign for the picture against my half-hearted memory of it, felt vindicated. I was extremely grateful that he had pushed Coogan so hard, and stimulated that remarkable interview. But somehow we had to overcome the Maginot line of Mo Rothman.

David wrote several times to his office, but received no reply. Meanwhile, Rachel Ford agreed that we could look at more of the private material, and we met her on 18 May 1978 at the Savoy. David drove us down to Denham, but traffic hold-ups ate into our screening time. With the memory of Miss Ford snapping at me for asking for too much, I was very reticent when she took me to the vault. Not wanting to blow this delicate situation, I accepted the minimum number of cans. I spotted a can marked HARRY LAUDER, and guessed this must be the film made for Harry Lauder's Fund for Wounded Soldiers in 1918. I asked if we could see it, and Miss Ford said "I'd prefer you to have that". I took some more visitor's reels, and two Lauder reels (which proved a mistake; they were simply short out-takes wrapped up individually).

Nothing could match the first experience, but this footage was equally fascinating. The first visitor was Max Eastman, a young socialist writer[10] who was a close friend of Chaplin's. A tall, blond man in a tweed suit, he stands with Chaplin in front of a fruit tree. Chaplin projects enormous vitality and good humour in all these visitor scenes; in this he giggles and picks fruit from the tree, handing one to Eastman, who puts the stone in his top pocket. Chaplin gobbles on the stone and pretends he can't swallow or open his mouth. Finally he and Eastman throw the stones at the lens. Benny Leonard, the champion boxer from New York's East Side, was a hero to all Jewish kids. (He is a leading character in Budd Schulberg's memoirs *Moving Pictures*.) He, his manager, Charlie and Syd Chaplin gather on the set of *A Dog's Life* and stage a cod boxing match. It all goes at a terrific pace and is very funny; Chaplin points energetically to take Benny Leonard's eye off target, and then wallops him.

A visit by Winston Churchill took place eleven years later, on the set of *City Lights*. Chaplin, in a white track suit, looks older, greyer and more reposed. Churchill and his party stand around self-consciously. Chaplin seems stuck for an idea to bring the visit to life. Suddenly he darts forward and performs a little dance, which converts a potentially

---

10. Both he, and Oona's father Eugene O'Neill, appear as characters in Warren Beatty's film *Reds* (1981).

Chaplin with Winston Churchill (r), Alf Reeves (l) and next to him, Churchill's son, Randolph, on the set of *City Lights*

dull and formal sequence into one of the most charming of the collection. But no, this scene was not Miss Ford's dance.

The Harry Lauder film proved to be what I had hoped: the split-reeler made for the wounded soldiers' fund, in 1918. It opened with a shot of Harry Lauder, wearing a kilt and playing the bagpipes, stomping down the sidewalk of La Brea Avenue, with the empty Hollywood Hills in the background. Chaplin comes out of the studio to greet him and they have a long conversation, in which Lauder gestures that he last saw him when he was "so high". On the open stage, Chaplin performs his walk to Lauder, and Lauder demonstrates his. Then they swap hats and do each other's walk. A scene was missing, then we saw a chase through the orange groves at the back of the studio. When they catch up with each other, they burst into laughter. Chaplin wipes Lauder's brow, sweeps the perspiration into his bowler hat and waters the plants.

When the individual rolls in the Lauder cans were joined up, they proved to be the rushes and out-takes. There were several scenes shot on the employment office set from *A Dog's Life*; in one of them, Lauder draws Chaplin's portrait with chalk on a blackboard. Chaplin objects to the size of his nose, and rubs it out and draws a shorter one. Lauder enlarges it again, and Chaplin makes a mock-Jewish gesture. At the end of this scene, Chaplin eats the chalk and Lauder follows suit. Then came a surprise, a candid moment of the two men rinsing their mouths out and laughing together in a corner of the set. Chaplin spits, then looks up and spots the cameraman and is obviously startled that he is still cranking. He yells at him, and one can lip-read "No, really, stop it!" He gestures energetically, but Totheroh cranks on. Finally, Sydney Chaplin walks up, grinning, and blocks the lens.

Chaplin thinks Harry Lauder has given him too large a nose

Scenes from the film made for the Harry Lauder Million Pound Fund for Maimed Men, Scottish Soldiers and Sailors

In the orchard, Lauder steals an apple. Chaplin catches him and, placing the apple on his head, levels a huge revolver at him. (This William Tell scene was finally used in *The Circus*.) Another surprise was a test from *City Lights* – the blind girl's vision of her mysterious admirer. Chaplin, dressed in a Russo-Ruritanian uniform, looked surprisingly impressive, if oddly camera-conscious. Films featuring handsome young officers were all the rage in the late twenties; this test suggested that Chaplin was modelling himself on John Gilbert.

"The only thing that's any use to you," said Miss Ford, "is the Jackie Coogan." I explained how useful the Harry Lauder film would be for our episode on War, and she did not object. So it was added to our little group of "snippets". "What I really wanted to find was the scene where he does the little dance,' she said. 'I'm sure it's in the spare takes of *The Circus*."

It was as well that the series was a long-term proposition, because negotiations with Mo Rothman for *The Kid* got nowhere. We were

Rollie Totheroh and Bell and Howell 2709s, the one on the right for the domestic negative, the one on the left (operated by Jack Wilson) for the foreign

permitted to put the sections we wanted on tape, but Miss Ford warned us that we should keep the length to the absolute minimum. Preferably two minutes. One by one, the *Hollywood* episodes were put together, and by November, we had a fairly respectable cut of "Comedy", which we had entitled *Comedy – a Serious Business*.

Miss Ford came down to Teddington again, and we showed her the roughcut in the theatre. She watched the episode without a word until we were thirty seconds into the Jackie Coogan sequence. "Too much of *The Kid*," she proclaimed. Disaster! It had been cut to the bone. When she had gone, and we were all shrouded in gloom, David and editor Dan Carter made some further incisions which were so skilful that they did not destroy the effect. Yet they were substantial enough to bring the length down. The sequence now ran 3 minutes 37 seconds. We had slowed the film down electronically to 20 fps. "At 24," said David, "it would be a mere two minutes fifty five seconds." That sounded a great deal better, so we passed the information to Rachel Ford in Vevey.

"Charlie never wanted *The Kid* slowed down," she said. "He'd be horrified." We learned later that she had ordered several of the Chaplin films to be stretch-printed, in an attempt to restore them to their original speed. But Chaplin disliked the effect so much that they were scrapped. None except *The Idle Class* and parts of *The Chaplin Revue* (*A Dog's Life*, *Shoulder Arms* and *The Pilgrim*) remained stretched (to their detriment).[11]

There was no set speed for silent films, although sixteen frames per second was the average in the early years. Comedies were invariably speeded up. Chaplin used to shoot some scenes at what he called "a happy fourteen", but he knew projectionists would speed up their machines as soon as they laced up one of his pictures. Camera speeds steadily increased during the twenties as the average speed of projection increased, and Chaplin's later films *The Gold Rush, The Circus* – can be projected at 24 fps without looking absurd. We explained to Miss Ford that the "slowing down" of *The Kid* helped the film rather than hindered it, for the sequences we had chosen were emotional rather than comic. She accepted what we told her, and, more importantly, accepted the length.

---

11. David Shepard put out laserdiscs in the US with the stretched sections replaced.

But we still faced the problem of Mo Rothman. We were immensely relieved when Mo's son Keith came to see us. His charm, enthusiasm and helpfulness softened our mental image of his father as a cross between Howard Hughes and General Ludendorff. He said his father knew that Oona supported the project, and was convinced there would be no further problems. He was spectacularly wrong. And he was as embarrassed as we were shaken. Mo Rothman demanded $5,000 for the sequence, with world rights and a ten-year license. Then Keith had to adjust the conditions: the $5,000 was for one UK showing only. Our average price per minute was $1,000. David had to deal with all this, since I am innumerate. And it placed the whole Chaplin section in jeopardy. Eventually David concluded a deal with Rothman, but it was a hard grind.

The comedy episode of Hollywood was completed, with Carl Davis re-recording the Chaplin music from *The Kid*, and it turned out to be among the most emotional moments in the entire series. When we dubbed it, in July 1979, Freddie Slade, the dubbing mixer, reached for his handkerchief. "It still works, doesn't it?" he said, dabbing his eyes.

The following month, the BBC presented Barry Norman's *Hollywood Greats*, a series about the private lives of the stars. The first was Chaplin. Both David and I detested it. Apart from an astonishingly cavalier attitude towards the material – scruffy 16mm dupes, covered in dirt and scratches – there was a *News of the World* prurience which we found maddening. Barry Norman purported to focus on the statue, but spent all his time leering at the feet of clay. Our reaction was hyper-critical. Reading the transcript of the programme recently I found it milder and more balanced than I remembered. But this sort of unreasonable attitude is often useful for creative people; it spurs them to action, just as a contentious letter in the *Times* spurs a flock of passionate rebuttals. Certainly, Barry Norman's programme was one of the strongest reasons why I thought we should do a proper study of Chaplin. I remember visiting Laurence Irving, the artist, who had been an art director in Hollywood at the end of the silents. He had known Chaplin, and Norman's programme upset him even more than us. A couple of months later, David and I went to visit Irving again. We planned to interview him for the episode on the coming of sound. He showed us some snapshots he had taken of Chaplin as "the Spirit of the World", clowning

'The Spirit of the World': wearing Mary Pickford's costume from *Pollyanna*, Chaplin is about to place the German helmet on the globe

in Mary Pickford's dress outside Pickfair. He held a globe, and, in an obvious foretaste of *The Great Dictator*, he surmounted it with a German army *Pickelhaube*. *Hollywood* was delayed by a three-month ITV strike. It eventually went out in January 1980, and its thirteen weekly episodes lasted until April. We worked on the last episodes while the first were going out. *Hollywood* had been such an enormous undertaking that I could not imagine any other project being necessary. If we ever reached the end, I thought, we would be sustained by sheer euphoria, a couple of superannuated producers basking on our laurels until the end of time. Actually, once the moment of completion arrived, we both began to think of the next project, and we both arrived at the same idea: "It's got to be Chaplin, hasn't it?" We knew what that decision entailed. We knew we would have to go back to Miss Ford, and start negotiations all over again. But we also knew that we could pay a proper tribute to Chaplin – something we were not able to do in *Hollywood*.

The question we had to ask ourselves was whether, in all the material we had seen, there was enough for a programme. That there was enough, in terms of footage, was undeniable. But programmes do not depend on length alone. There has to be shape, there has to be structure, there has to be a point to it all. It would not be enough to join one splendid sequence after another, and say "Look what we've found!" So our approach to Miss Ford was a curious one. On one hand, we were anxious to make the programme. On the other, we were not sure about the material, and wanted to see it all. She said what she always said: "I shall have to ask Oona."

For our first meeting with Oona, we were invited to the circus. Not an ordinary circus, but something called *Le Cirque Imaginaire*, which was being staged at the Riverside Theatre, Hammersmith. Victoria Chaplin, her husband Jean-Baptiste Thierry and their two children were the only performers, together with some doves, and a rabbit. It all sounded insufferably twee, and since I enjoyed neither the circus nor the theatre I was not looking forward to it. This time, not only were David and I invited, but also our wives, Pauline and Virginia. And I was surprised to encounter the American director Robert Parrish. This was useful, because he had been one of the kids in *City Lights*, and he would be a valuable eyewitness for our film. Oona arrived with her childhood friend Gloria Vanderbilt.

If one wanted to cast a woman who had spent her adult life married to an old man, who had borne him eight children, and had ten grandchildren, one would settle for a prematurely aged creature of vast size – an earth mother. We knew Oona was nothing like that, but it was a trifle disconcerting to meet the woman herself, and to find her still so girlish she could almost have been her own eldest daughter. Small, with narrow but bright eyes, a broad forehead which looked worried whenever she wrinkled her brow, she had an enchanting smile. She laughed a lot – mostly through nervousness – and moved in sharp and sudden gestures. Gloria Vanderbilt, every inch the aristocratic American, monopolized her for most of the evening. The show proved to be one of the most exciting things I had seen in the theatre. Full of imagination, and wit, it was as delicate as a Japanese watercolour and as hard to describe. Victoria Chaplin said not a word throughout the entire performance; she was as expressive and graceful and daring as a silent comedian. Jean-Baptiste, with wild hair and conspiratorial grin, was a perfect counterpart. We were delighted and relieved that the show was so good and that our enthusiasm could be genuine. That same evening, Rachel Ford suggested a scheme to get us to Switzerland.

Boxer Benny Leonard with Chaplin, 1918

4. To Switzerland

If only it had been a few years ago! I had always dreamed of driving up to Chaplin's house at Vevey, in Switzerland. But Chaplin had to be there. He had to say "I didn't realise you were so interested. I have some unusual film in the vault that has never been seen before... " Well, it had happened in a way, thanks to Rachel Ford. David and I flew to Geneva, and took a train to Vevey, where we booked in to the Hotel Trois Couronnes. Our rooms looked out on to Lac Léman (Lake Geneva), which, with its backdrop of mountains and swans and yachts dotting its surface, was so picturesque we burst out laughing.

Miss Ford called for us in a green Volkswagen station wagon and drove us inland. She pointed to where the tall, thin concrete stanchions of an *autoroute* viaduct rose from a valley. "The Chaplin woods are there – marvellous trees frequently visited by experts – and they built the *autoroute* just outside it," she sniffed in disgust, but took advantage of the motorway. She left by the Corsier exit and drove up a drive, thickly overhung with trees. Le Manoir de Ban was a handsome building in the French style of 1835. Miss Ford led us through some of the rooms. Beyond a trio of Oscars and some other trophies, no one could have guessed that Chaplin had lived there. We were shown what Miss Ford described as a "ghastly" sofa, a worn, pink couch of no particular distinction until she told us it had featured in *City Lights*. There was none of the paraphernalia of a film maker – no signed pictures, no souvenirs. The interior was surprisingly ornate and rococo. The view through the French windows was soothing – a vast, freshly-mown lawn, a line of tulips in Swiss red and white on parade at the foot of a colonnaded terrace. The white pillars were carved with dark red rambler roses. As we were led round the corner, we saw a beautiful old barn with an open end packed with logs. Over the garage was a flat, its windows decorated with locally-wrought metalwork which incorporated the initials "CC" and walking sticks. As we walked through an orchard, there seemed to be the atmosphere of an English country house, with the Hollywood touch of a mountain in the distance. A steep hill and a kitchen garden led to a thick wood, beyond which cowbells could be heard.

The object of the trip was to try to convince Oona that our project was a good idea. But the drawback to social events like this is that important issues are avoided by common consent. Clarissa and James Mason, who lived at nearby Corseaux, came to dinner, as did the Chaplin's youngest son, Christopher, aged 17. He bore a startling resemblance to the young Chaplin in *How to Make Movies*. By the time we returned to the sitting room, and the *City Lights* sofa, we were beginning to give up hope. Miss Ford did her best to prepare everyone to look at the comedy episode of *Hollywood* which we had brought on cassette, but the conversation went off at a tangent and the opportunity was lost.

Oona brought up the subject of her new apartment in New York, and out came the plans. I looked across at David and he looked glum. Just as we were leaving, however, Oona, with that sixth sense she so often displayed, said "But you had a project... " David started to say, "There was no time..." I jumped in: "Well, let's put it very briefly... " And I took a deep breath and David began explaining: "We were not able to do justice to Chaplin in the series for reasons we are all aware of, and we felt a marvellous way of making up for it would be to show the unpublished Chaplin..." "Oh, wouldn't it?" said Oona.

Miss Ford drove us back to the hotel, and *en route* said, "Of course, it all depends on whether Oona likes the programme. If she doesn't, you're cooked."

5. Another Think Coming

We knew Raymond Rohauer had some rare Chaplin material. During the making of *Hollywood* he had revealed a superb print of *The Bond*, a one-reeler Chaplin had made for the Fourth Liberty Loan campaign in World War One. The film had been lost until Rohauer had rediscovered it, although how he found it was a subject he kept rather quiet about. He also had a reel of Chaplin "personal material" which included part of the visit by Maxine Elliott. At one of his meetings with Rohauer, David talked of our plans for the Chaplin programme. "How much footage does she have that hasn't been seen before?" asked Rohauer. David wasn't sure. He made a guess. "About thirty thousand feet." "Is that all?" said Rohauer. "I've got more than that." "More than that of what?" "Chaplin material that hasn't been seen before." "Why didn't you tell us?"

And Rohauer came out with one of his favourite phrases: "You didn't ask." "What sort of material is it?" "What if I told you that it was rushes from the Mutuals?" David could not believe his ears. And yet Rohauer had never talked of having a film he could not produce. "How much footage do you think you have?" "Guess." "Well, fifty thousand feet?" "More." "A hundred thousand?" "More." "Two hundred thousand?" "Maybe." "What does that represent?" "Maybe all." David was stunned. He told me later that he thought, "Wait till I get back and tell Kevin." He used to get a double kick from those meetings with Rohauer; hearing the revelations at first hand, and then rushing back to tell me, and watching my eyes pop.

The importance of the Mutual rushes would be incalculable to any study of Chaplin. In 1916, the Mutual Film Corporation had tempted Chaplin away from Essanay with an offer unprecedented in the history of entertainment; they would pay him $670,000 a year, plus a bonus, in return for twelve two-reel comedies. They built him a studio, on Lillian Way, Los Angeles, which they called The Lone Star Studio (it later passed to Buster Keaton). Here he produced what many historians consider his finest work – films like *The Cure, The Immigrant, Behind the Screen, Easy Street* and *The Adventurer*. He made them remarkably swiftly – one film every month, although some took longer and the series of twelve consumed sixteen months.

When David told me the news, I was as astonished as he expected. But, being the pessimist of the partnership, I was also full of doubt. Why, when Rohauer knew that we'd been hard at work for years on a series about the silent cinema, had he not revealed the existence of this material before? I was frankly sceptical and I expected the next few months to be enlivened by a series of false alarms. The trouble with Rohauer was that he was in London so rarely, and for such short visits. David dutifully met him at his favourite hotel, the Mayfair, each time he came. At one of these meetings, it became apparent that the first problem over the Mutual rushes was their whereabouts. I must admit that I laughed up my sleeve when David told me, straight-faced, that he didn't think even Rohauer knew where they were. They were probably in France. At once, my mind jumped to the obvious conclusion: he had deposited them with the Cinematheque Francaise, the French film archive, in the days of its flamboyant and unreliable director, Henri Langlois. The greatest collector in the world – he even had the edge on Rohauer – Langlois was the worst archivist. His precious material was kept in atrocious conditions, and he had had several fires. The last great Cinematheque fire destroyed an estimated 7,000 prints. If Rohauer genuinely had had the Mutual rushes, the chances were strong that he didn't have them now. When Rohauer began hinting that he would like an advance, David told him: "The whole thing sounds fantastic, the most exciting find in the world. But in no way can we begin to think of talking seriously about it until we actually see the footage. It's no good my going to Thames Television and saying Rohauer's got a lot of Chaplin stuff and we want to make a programme out of it. We've got to see it."

On their subsequent meetings, they simply discussed the best ways of our seeing the footage – once the footage had been located. My suspicions told me that Rohauer was on to a good thing. Having produced all that rare footage for *Hollywood*, we were forced to take him seriously. Whenever he came to London, he had someone to talk to. He could involve David in a great deal of work tracking down clues and dealing with the intransigent French on his behalf. Rohauer would use David to help him recover his collection, much of which he had deposited with the Cinematheque. Among it would be perhaps three cans of Mutual rushes, as a sort of sop.

However, I had to admit that even three cans of Mutual rushes were worth all the trouble he could throw at us. The real problems would start when David was confronted by the Cinematheque. In February 1968, Henri Langlois resigned from his post in an angry gesture against the government. Culture Minister Andre Malraux objected to the chaos, and wanted it put in order. The world's filmmakers saw the victimisation of a great lover of the cinema and they lined up on Langlois' side. The government eventually backed down, and Langlois returned to run the Cinematheque until his death. But during the time he thought the government would take over, he began squirrelling the vast collection into secret deposits which only he and his closest associate, Mme Meerson, knew about.

6. 'I Never Give Interviews'

Thames Television had lost £700,000 because of the strike. On 9 June 1980, David and I had a meeting with our head of documentaries, Mike Wooller, to discuss our future projects. The company had few enough documentary slots before the strike; now they had even fewer, so there was no sense that we had to rush something out. The Chaplin idea seemed a good one, but we had to go to America to check on who was left from the early days. We decided to leave in a week. The following day, David and I met Miss Ford at the Savoy and told her that it looked as though the Chaplin project was on. For the first time David brought up the name of Raymond Rohauer, explaining that he had worked with us on *Hollywood*. "Don't mention that name," she said. "It gives me nettle rash. When I think of the money Charlie spent suing him and the time I spent... The legal documents fill cupboards. He is the last man in the world I would want associated with Chaplin. I wouldn't allow his name on the same credits." When David pointed out that he had only come up with Mutual material, which was out of copyright, she declared "He has a perfect right to that. I mean to say, Charlie had the chance of buying that back and he wanted nothing to do with it. In a way it's his fault that it fell into that man's hands. But if I find that he has a foot of the copyright films, I've got him." "What will you do?" "Why sue him of course," she said, with a beatific smile. As she picked up her handbag and prepared to leave, Rachel added, "Of course, it's nothing to do with me. You'll have to ask Oona." Pause. "And of course, she'll agree. She agrees to everything."

17 June 1980: David and I flew to New York and had lunch with Raymond Rohauer. I was surprised at how relaxed, even humorous, he was in David's company. However, the fact that I was still *persona non grata* was emphasised when the business talks began and I was expected to leave.

As soon as David and I reached Los Angeles we began hunting. Lisa Mitchell, a journalist, proved very helpful and gave us the names of several people who were interested in Chaplin. While David made a business trip to a local TV station, I sat by the telephone and made a concerted effort to reach anyone who might have had anything to do with Chaplin. It was very strange what little headway I made. Silent star

Carmel Myers (*Ben-Hur*) said she hardly knew him. Sidney Skolsky, journalist and reportedly a friend of Chaplin's, snapped, "You'd waste your journey." I remembered, when we were shooting *Hollywood*, that Olive Carey suggested we met Virginia Cherrill, the blind girl in *City Lights*. Now she gave me her number, and full of trepidation I rang her.

"I never give interviews," she said bluntly. "I felt very bitterly about Chaplin's attitude to British War Relief. When we asked if we could have the premiere of *Great Dictator* to raise funds for British War Relief, he refused to give it." "What about *City Lights*?" "I have very fond memories of all the crew. Charlie and I didn't get on terribly well. I had not been an actress before and it was a constant wrangle. I have unpleasant memories of all that. I do promise you I don't want to be interviewed," she added. "I've been ill and I'm very busy with charity work." She did, however, agree to a meeting later in our visit.

I rang Georgia Hale, the leading lady of *The Gold Rush*, and she was just going out. She said she had fond memories of Chaplin, but she didn't want to be photographed. I then called Tim Durant, a friend of Chaplin from the 1930s; although he never worked on any of the films, he became an official of United Artists. "Is that Tim Durant?" "It could be." "This is Kevin Brownlow, from London." "Obviously."

I arranged to meet him at a most unusual rendezvous, a presbyterian church in Beverly Hills. Durant was a tall, handsome man in his late seventies, who had become famous in England as the Galloping Grandad when he took part in the Grand National in his late sixties. He looked a little like Abraham Lincoln in an old movie. He talked amusingly and vividly, and David recorded him on a miniature Sony tape recorder he had just bought in New York. We sat in a cool, shaded courtyard attached, mission-style, to the church. (Durant made sure we contributed to church funds before we left.) Durant warned us that he was doing a book on his relationship with Chaplin and he didn't want to give too much away on television. However, he told us a great deal, although necessarily very little about the way Chaplin worked.

Tim Durant

I met Charlie when he returned from a trip round the world with Paulette Goddard. I had been a great fan of his, and I would rather meet him than anybody in Hollywood. But it seemed impossible because when he did return from this trip, he became a recluse. He was sort of upset about things, I guess. I went to a great many Hollywood parties and he was never there. But one day King Vidor called me up. I used to play tennis with King quite a bit, and he said, "Look, Tim, are you free to play some doubles today?" And I said, "Sure." So he picked me up and I said, "Where are we going?" He said "We're going up to Chaplin's." So I played some doubles with Chaplin and Bill Tilden. I started to play and I froze. I never played worse in my life, and I was so excited to meet him, because he was everything I expected him to be. He was graceful, he was the most marvellous host, he was full of life and spirit, and keen and interested in whoever he was talking to. That tennis friendship developed into a permanent job with him at the United Artists studio where I represented him as a member of the United Artists.

He really lived on the response of people. If you could talk and if he could talk to you and you were interested, he'd fasten on you. I was a wonderful audience for him, and even if he repeated it many times, he was so perfect in his timing and his imagination and his ebullience and enthusiasm that I was absolutely held by him every time that he walked out on stage, so to speak. I was always there, you see. That's what brought us close together. He tried out a lot of things on me. I think he would have tried out the same things on you – your reactions would probably have been as good, if not better. But he had me there and I was a captive audience, and a willing captive, and I was always there with a remark. Very often I would tell him what I thought, and usually his reaction was, "No, no Tim, that stinks, that stinks." The next day he would bring it up as his own idea, without realising it. So I treated him with great respect and deference and he knew that I was fond of him, and he knew that I thought he was a genius – which he was. When you think of it, he could do everything – he could not only write, direct, he could do the choreography, he wrote the music, he cut the picture, he financed it, he starred in it and he did the casting. He did everything, and of course it took him a long time to do it.

He dictated quite a bit of *The Great Dictator* to me when we were up at Pebble Beach. Charlie wanted to do like Shaw did, you know, take a serious subject and do it with humour. He wanted to destroy Hitler by making him look ridiculous. Charlie saw many of Hitler's newsreels. He said, "This guy is one of the greatest actors I've ever seen." Hitler would pick up a child, once in a while, and be very loving, and Charlie admired his acting. He made a speech about humanity and there was a great argument about that. It didn't belong in there, it should not be connected with the picture. It was unaesthetic to have Charlie go out there and propagandise. The film salesmen told you, "You'll lose a million dollars in rentals for that," and he said, "I don't care if it's five million, I'm going to do it because it's on my mind." So he did it, and it did cost him quite a bit of business. A lot of people said, "What the hell, I didn't come here to listen to somebody getting on his soap box." It affected the critics, particularly. They said it wasn't right so strongly that people, thinking it was a propaganda picture, didn't go[12].

At parties, he was always the centre of attention. I saw this happen more than once, people like Noel Coward, three or four other great names, he would walk

---

12. Nonetheless, it made twice as much as any other Chaplin film.

in and they would all make way for Charlie. He would take over right away, the centre of attention, and of course he loved that. His drawing room stuff at parties was every bit as good as what he did in his pictures, and sometimes even better. Because he had a live audience – which he didn't get in his pictures. He was magnificent.

That night we met Steffi Sidney, the daughter of Sidney Skolsky and a Chaplin devotee. She said her father was not too well, which was probably why he claimed to know nothing. By coincidence, a local cable television station was transmitting several Chaplin films, *Pay Day*, *A Dog's Life* and *The Pilgrim*, and we watched them on her TV. For tomorrow, we were to meet Dean Riesner, who played the obnoxious kid in *The Pilgrim*. Riesner was the son of Charles "Chuck" Riesner, a former vaudeville man, author of the wartime song *Goodbye Broadway, Hello France* and later a successful comedy director (he co-directed with Buster Keaton as well as Chaplin, and directed Charlie's brother Sydney). Dean Riesner was extremely friendly and helpful and, considering he was only a four-year-old at the time, he remembered a great deal about *The Pilgrim*. He told us that he was such a gentle child that he had no desire to hit "Uncle Charlie", which was what the scene called for. The irony is that Riesner had written several of the most violent Clint Eastwood pictures, including *Magnum Force* and *Dirty Harry*!

Dean Riesner

My father and Chaplin had a good, close relationship. He was an assistant director for the first couple of films and then Chaplin made him an associate director. They would argue a great deal about gags, both having been in vaudeville and they both knew audience reactions. My father was a "Let's go get 'em" kind of a man and Chaplin was a great cogitator and one day they were filming a picture out in the street, and they were trying to get a gag about a manhole. I think my father was willing to settle for anything, but it wasn't going well for Chaplin and they had a terrific argument about it. My father finally got mad and stormed off, and he went down the street to Poverty Row, and he got another job almost instantly. The picture my father did was a two-reeler, it took three days to shoot and each morning he'd go past Chaplin – Chaplin was still cogitating. He finished the picture and went back to Charlie and said, "I've finished the picture and I'd like to go back to work for you." And Charlie said, "Fine, Chuck, fine, but you're absolutely wrong about this joke and I'll tell you why." And they started the argument on the same spot where my father had quit three days before.

Charlie had a dictionary in his office. He was a man who liked to use big words on people. He would look these words up in the dictionary and he'd come out and spring them on the guys in the crew. And one day they got together to frame him. They got his dictionary and they looked up a word and they said, "Charlie, you know the main trouble with you is that you're a quidnunc." And they walked off, and Charlie couldn't wait to get back to his dictionary to see what the hell they'd called him. And as he goes for the dictionary, they're all looking through the window, and they'd left a little note – "Hi, Charlie" – under the word "quidnunc".

Making a picture in those days was very much a home-cooking proposition. In other words, if you needed a kid to play in the thing, you'd say, "Who's got a kid?" and they'd bring one down. I lived up on Franklin Circle with my family and they needed a kid to play the brat in this picture *(The Pilgrim)*, doing a lot of slapping and a lot of kicking and a lot of torturing of poor Charlie, and my old man brings me down. I was a well-brought-up kid, and a gentle child, and I was not a great slapper of people. And so when it came time to start slapping people, I didn't want to do it. "I don't want to hit Uncle Charlie", and poor Charlie couldn't get me to slap him until finally he and Sydney were playing slapping games. And they'd say, "Oh, I love to be slapped. I just adore being slapped," and he'd say, "Sydney, hit me again," and Sydney would give him a shot and Charlie would say, "Ho, ho, this is so much fun. I just love it!" and wham – hitting himself. He finally convinced me that slapping was a great charge to him. I saw the picture recently and it's a really weird sensation to see yourself that young, and all these things came back to me. I remember, for instance, I was supposed to grab a goldfish out of a goldfish bowl and put it down his neck. If you ever try to grab a goldfish out of a goldfish bowl, the best of luck to you. I don't know how the hell you do it. So I'm trying to grab this thing and I can't get it and so they had Granville Redmond, an artist in residence – he was a deaf and dumb man who lived at the studio – he carved a goldfish out of a carrot, and they put this carrot goldfish in there. I was waiting for the gag when I saw the picture, but it wasn't there. The carrot goldfish didn't do, I imagine.

And then, at the end, I saw Charlie finally getting his revenge on this kid who was torturing him to death, and he runs up and kicks him in the ass and sends him rolling down the corridor. I don't remember ever getting kicked like that. And then I remembered that it was little Billy, a midget, who doubled me in that shot and I remember my father bringing him home the night before, and they were both drunk, smoking cigars. And I was bringing out my toys and showing them to this midget.

I also remember the flypaper. They finally torture me at the end of this picture, because nothing would do, I was really giving poor Charlie hell. But that flypaper I still remember. It was not a comfortable thing. They used real flypaper – they don't have fake flypaper, you know. I still haven't gotten it all off.

When I was up behind him at the fishbowl, I said, "Why don't I put water on you? You must put your hand out and think it's raining." And they used the gag, so I was one of the youngest gag men in the history of the world.

He treated me as an equal. He was very kind and patient. He was very thoughtful and affectionate. Generally, they'd block out a scene and try for whatever they were going for in the gag. He had a man named Earl Taylor, who had a harmonium to give background music to the scene. They wouldn't go with the one take, they would print an awful lot of film, because it was the cheapest thing they had.

He was a stubborn man, and if it wasn't working for him, he would become very morose and fretful and he would become difficult to live with. He had a big prop room. He used to buy out second hand stores – just buy the whole thing and put it into his prop room and he would look and there would be a funny looking little teakettle or something like that, and he would notice it and he would think what if he put a nipple on the end of that spout for feeding the baby with?

We decided to drive to Santa Barbara to visit Olive Carey, the widow of Harry Carey. While we were there, we hoped for a chance to see Virginia Cherrill. I rang her first. She allowed a sliver of hope: "Are you going to see Ollie (Carey) anyway?"

"Yes!" I said.

"Well, call me again at 4.30."

Two hours later, we reached Ollie Carey's and relaxed in her enchanting company until the appointed time. Then Ollie made the call for us – no answer. She called several times thereafter. Nothing. She was, however, able to leave a message and, an hour or so later, as we prepared to leave, the phone rang.

"Where the hell have you been?" asked Ollie. The doctor's, apparently.

Ollie began to persuade her to see us. We could sense her resistance. "Listen, David and Kevin are the nicest people you could meet" (David and Kevin exchanged rueful glances) "and they aren't about to take you for a ride. If they could just call in and talk to you for ten minutes, they'd be tickled to death."

She'd done it. She got us John Wayne for *Hollywood*, and she got us Virginia Cherrill for *Chaplin*.

We drove round for our ten-minute talk, and we stayed two and a half hours. Virginia Cherrill lived with her husband, Florian Martini, Polish air ace of World War II, in a small but expensive house with a white gate. It was a white, wood-framed bungalow, with a picture window giving on to a square garden enclosed by tall trees and bushes and palms. There was a rather scorched lawn. The house was furnished with great care – the hall had memories of Virginia Cherrill's days as Countess Jersey – engravings of Henry VII's Richmond Palace, Osterley Park, Kew Palace.

She was a very handsome woman. She wore sensible, elegant and English clothes, and grey hair, without that blue rinse American matrons are famous for. She said she loved people who gave her a laugh, which made her difficult relationship with Chaplin all the sadder. But she didn't take film making or acting seriously, and evidently couldn't understand those who did.

Virginia Cherrill

I came to California on a visit and was taken to the prize fights by my uncle, who was an invalid, and was allowed to sit in his wheelchair at the end of the first row. And I sat next to a small man in white flannels, with very brown skin and very white hair and my uncle knew him and so he introduced me, and it was Chaplin. But I didn't believe him because Chaplin to me meant the Tramp.

The next day, my uncle phoned me and said that Charlie had asked us to lunch at the beach on Saturday. So this sounded great fun. We went to a beach house and, as we went in the door, there were two men standing in the front hall, Charlie and a tall man who looked like

Fernandel, who said, "That's the girl I've been telling you about." And Charlie said, "No, that's the girl I've been telling *you* about." It seems that Henri d'Abbadie d'Arrast, who was the tall man, had seen me at the Ambassador Hotel, where I was staying, and had said, "Charlie, there's a girl at the hotel – I've seen her – she's blind." (I'm so short sighted. I really can't see at all.) And Charlie had paid no attention.

He asked me if I'd like to do the film, and asked me to come to the studio, where he made tests without my glasses, and evidently he decided I was the person to play the blind girl. I was given some makeup and told to put it on – there was no makeup man. I think I must have looked absolutely dreadful. I can't think how I ever got the part. But this was always a problem for me, the makeup, because I'm sure I never looked the same two days running, and the same with hairdressing. We had no hairdresser at the studio and my hair grew from a rather close shingle to shoulder length during the picture, which was supposed to be over a short period of time. But nobody minded. Charlie said that if the mood was right, nobody would notice. Before I signed my contract with Charlie, I made very clear that I wasn't an actress, that I'd had no training of any kind and he said, "That's exactly what I want. If you had had any training you would have to unlearn it because I like to work my own way and it's not the way anyone else works."

The company had to be there, ready to work, made up at nine o'clock, but Charlie came if he felt like it, if there was no tennis going or if it wasn't raining, then he might come every day for months and months, but we never knew. Because one waited sometimes for hours, sometimes for days, sometimes for months – virtually three or four months and Charlie wouldn't come to the studio. Occasionally, we'd call the house and ask if he'd left – this was the tactful way to put it – and if we were told he was playing tennis or something, we knew it was safe to go home. But as we had no restaurant in the studio and nothing to do, I simply sat in my dressing room and read books, knitted, did needlepoint and was generally bored. I often tried to sneak out of the studio, until I was caught. I'd been out with a beau for lunch, and I was ten minutes late, thinking he wasn't coming – but he came that day. After that, I was never allowed to leave the studios in the morning. I lunched every day after that in the bungalow with Charlie and Henry Bergman and visitors. Usually I was the only girl, but it was interesting and he had a very good cook. Charlie adored entertaining and if there was a musician present, he was a musician. If there was a writer present he was a writer. He told us of his childhood – going to the park and seeing the pretty children. He remembered colours and he said they were all so beautifully dressed in pink and blue and yellow, with their nannies – he seemed almost as if he were talking about toys that he couldn't afford to have. It made a great impression on him. He told us that he was very poor and he went to some school for poor children and it was terribly cold and they tore chairs apart and burned them on the bathroom floor. He was punished for that.

His one extravagance – he didn't care how many takes he took. In fact, I often thought that if he couldn't think what he was going to do next, he simply went on doing the same shot over again until he thought of it. But he was a perfectionist, and to us it often seemed to be exactly the same, but to him it was not. I think he must have shot enough film to sink the Queen Mary, but he'd take it over and over again and when he'd finally say "It's a take," we'd breathe a sigh of relief and he'd say, "Well, perhaps just once more."

He was a great inspiration. He gave you so much of the spirit of what he was trying to get out of you. He acted out every part, this was his way of directing. We had no script, and Charlie would simply say, "In this scene, I want you to do so-and-so," and then he would show you exactly how he wanted it done. And it sounds ridiculous, but you found yourself feeling that he was you. How could he be a blind girl? But he was – if he handed you a flower, you had this feeling that he was that person. He might grow impatient if he couldn't get what he wanted, but he was patient with me, I was a complete beginner. I'd never been an actress. I'd never read lines. We didn't read lines the way one does nowadays, but if he wanted a scene where I was speaking he would make me say it and so it had to be felt. I often found myself laughing when I shouldn't have done, or breaking up, because he was very naughty. It was a sort of pixie thing – he really liked breaking people up. He would do something that I wasn't expecting and I hadn't enough experience to ad-lib over it so I simply cracked up. I didn't know enough to judge my performance. It never occurred to me to judge my performance. If Charlie wasn't pleased, I heard about it.

Charlie fired me in the middle of the film. I was late coming back, probably from lunch, and he was kept waiting, which was not allowed, so he said I was spoiled and obviously shouldn't be in films and I was fired. So I went to the Hearst ranch for a holiday. Marion Davies was a darling and very kind and hospitable, not only to me but to everyone. And she loved making mischief. So I was feeling rather low and she said, "Don't worry. You're not really fired. Charlie'll have you back because he will never waste all that film," and she was quite right. After a couple of weeks he phoned and said, "Why aren't you at work?" So I said, "You remember – you fired me." But he said, "Come back down here, behave yourself, get back to work." So Marion said, "Wait a minute. You had your 21st birthday while you were here, your contract's no good. You can get more money." So as I had signed with the studio for $75 a week, which was not very much money, even in those days, although to me it was quite impressive, I said, "How much shall I ask for?" She said "At least double." So I said to Charlie, "I can't come back and work because I no longer have a contract with you." He said, "What do you mean?" I said "I signed it before

I was of age." He said, "That's nonsense, absolute nonsense." I said, "No it isn't. I was 21 last week and ask your lawyer if it's not so." He hung up. He called back later and said, "I think you'd better come down and we'll talk about it." So Marion said, "Now you've got him." And I went back and I got double the amount – I had the large sum of $150 a week from then on, for the rest of the film.

I'm afraid I wasn't very dedicated. To be an actress one must be willing to make tremendous sacrifices. I've known actors who have made tremendous sacrifices, whose whole life was acting, who would do anything to be a success – and I never felt that way. I don't think Charlie really liked me very much. I don't know why. I liked him. I was very impressed with him. But we had almost no

Virginia Cherrill in (endless) rehearsals for *City Lights*

social contact of any kind. I was never invited to his house because he didn't entertain very much, but when he did entertain, I wasn't invited. I had been married and divorced and perhaps I was more sophisticated than – perhaps he saw me as the blind girl, and not as me, and for this reason didn't like me.

Charlie was a god, you forget. Everyone forgets that in the studio he was the only person whose opinion mattered in any way. There was no such thing as criticism, or suggestions, unless he asked for it. Suggestions – he never asked for criticism. I think he listened to Harry Crocker and Harry d'Arrast, because they were friends, and perhaps his equals, he felt. Whereas the rest of us were peons.

My main memory of the boxing match is that he enjoyed it so much that it went on and on, day after day, week after week. We had a marvellous time. Everybody in town came to watch. Almost the only social life we had at the studio was the boxing match, because everybody loved boxing in Hollywood in those days, and it was so funny and he thoroughly enjoyed it. I think the scene that gave us the most problems was the recognition scene at the end. Because it had to be believable and this worried him a great deal. A lot of people thought it was the introductory scene where the rich man drove up and I mistook Charlie for him, but I feel it was the scene at the end.

I had a feeling that Charlie was very insecure and perhaps this accounted for his ego – his always being on show, always the entertainer. He didn't want people, perhaps, to know the real Charlie. One's bound to be insecure with a childhood like his. Charlie had to be first in everything. If there were stars present, he had to be the most important star. Charlie was always acting, he was always "on". He could play anyone – he could be me, he could be Marie Dressler (he was wonderful as Marie Dressler). He could be a Spanish dancer. It's curious – he was very inoffensive in his imitations and he was a marvellous mimic. Somehow, it was fun and amusing. It was a great experience in my life. I could wish that I'd had a happier relationship with Charlie.

After this fascinating experience, we drove back via Ollie Carey's to celebrate our collaboration in John Jameson.

The next day was the last on this initial research trip, so it was a relief to be able to see Georgia Hale. It was a boiling hot day, with the temperatures in the '90s. After a morning of phone calls, I was benumbed by the heat when we arrived at her little mock-Georgian house. I twisted the handle of the bell and the door was opened almost at once. There stood the kind of woman who might have run a Las Vegas bordello – a blonde wig of incredible flamboyance – curls bursting out all over – eyelashes like the crown on the Statue of Liberty – bus-red lipstick and a face that had been so lifted that the only wrinkles remaining were around the mouth. Her dress was a two-piece mauve bell-tent, with matching global earrings, and floppy trousers. She was very welcoming and said: "Isn't it hot – I'll get you a cold drink." And off she scurried to her kitchen. David and I exchanged "Oh my God" glances. The interior was as flamboyant and plastic as her exterior. There was a copy of the *Christian Science Monitor*, and a photo of herself when young in *Gold Rush* days on a side table. When David asked if he could use his recorder, she said, "Oh sure." I told her I remembered her from *Salvation Hunters*. "Oh, you know about that?" "I've seen it several times, you were extraordinary." And she still was. As we talked, I realised I was present at one of the most remarkable interviews I had ever listened to. The absurd war paint gradually disappeared. We were conscious only of an exceptional and courageous woman. She had never given interviews, she said. "But when I heard you were from London, and friends of Ivor Montagu, I thought, oh, I must see them. But when they ask me to go on the Merv Griffin show, which they do all the time – yuck."

It was an extraordinary sensation, sitting in front of this ridiculously over-made-up woman, and to hear the reminiscences flow with such intelligence and authenticity. It was uncanny. She really did look 45 from where I sat, a woman of the fifties and sixties, and it seemed impossible to hear such sharp recall of the twenties. It was like attending a séance and hearing the youthful medium talk fluently of a time before she was born. But it was all very well recording such an interview on a

The Gold Rush (1925) – Henri d'Abbadie d'Arrast, Eddie Manson, Chaplin, Rollie Totheroh, Chuck Riesner

pocket cassette machine; it was not even of broadcast quality. Would she repeat the same memories, in the same vivid style, when we came to film her? And equally important, would she agree to us filming her?

As we walked back to the car, I said, "That makes the whole trip worthwhile."

"She's so vivacious," said David. "Do you think she'll do it?" "I had the feeling, as I listened, that this was a time-of-a-lifetime experience, that it was so perfect that she'll never do it again. Either she'll refuse... or something will happen." "I didn't expect such a metaphysical answer," said David.

7. Whatever Next?

Shortly after we had returned from the United States, Rachel Ford telephoned me. She said that she had just come back from Vevey. We were anxious to know how Oona had reacted to the cassette of comedy. "When I arrived, Oona had still not seen your cassette, but Christopher (the youngest child) had, and he was raving about it. He said it was "beautifully done" and he was arranging to pinch James Mason's[13] copies so that he could see the whole lot. The upshot of all this is that Oona is now very keen on your making the programme using the private material. But I will want to know more about your project because I don't know much about it. And there are several other projects. You probably know about them. Of course, we cannot stop them, unless we made some publicity about Oona and the children being involved in your scheme."

Among the other projects: Lord Grade of ATV was planning a drama based on Chaplin's life; Home Box Office was doing a 45-minute documentary entirely devoted to Chaplin between 1911 and 1919, narrated by Joel Grey.

"I don't know what to do if you associate with Rohauer," she said. "I'll have to show you the documents I have." I told her that we had met Rohauer, and that he had offered to let us see the material, "when the weather got cooler, in October." She said she knew where it was stored in France. "He is supposed to have given back all the Chaplin material. If he produces anything of ours we would have him on hot toast."

I pleaded for the material. "He doesn't have your attitude towards preserving it. He has never copied it and the nitrate is even now probably decomposing. Thames could rescue it." "I would sue him immediately," she said. "The Chaplin name cannot be linked with Rohauer's." She said that nothing could be done, anyway, until she had talked to Mo Rothman, who was then in Budapest. "But we would like to put out some publicity in the press to say that your project had the wholehearted co-operation of Lady Chaplin." We were delighted by that, although we did not want to be used as a stick to beat other projects out of existence.

13. James Mason spoke the narration for *Hollywood*.

"Now where will you boys be on August 8th? If you'll be in London, I'll show you some more of the material." Just before ringing off, she returned to the subject of Rohauer: "I do sometimes rag. But I'm not ragging this time. I never want to see those names together without a 'v' between them."

When I told all this to David, his face fell. "August 8th?" he said. "I'll be on holiday. But you go. See if you think there is enough there."

The first few shots were a splendid *hors d'oeuvres* for the rest of this incredibly rich and rather indigestible meal. They showed the interior of Chaplin's laboratory. The photographic quality was first-class. Lab workers were shown hitching the film from racks on to vast drying drums, and setting them in motion. It looked primitive, but one had to remind oneself that the film one was watching had gone through this very process. Then came a series of shots of Chaplin directing. Richard Patterson had used them in *Gentleman Tramp*, and Chaplin himself had used them in *Chaplin Revue*. So they were not unknown. But to see them uncut, at their full length was fascinating. It was just a test; Chaplin was first seen putting the finishing touches to the actress's hair. He places her in front of the camera and acts out everything he wants – one moment he is coquettish, the next he is horrified, the next amused. She mimics his expressions, although one hardly noticed her – all eyes were on Chaplin at work in the cutting room, then he was back directing the girl again. There was no order: therein lay the piquant surprises!

A slow motion boxing match with Kid Lewis in the grounds of the studio was followed by a much funnier speeded-up version. At the end, Lewis and Chaplin ran into the distance, the speed changed to slow motion, and they performed a dance remarkably similar to the one which became a trademark for Morecambe and Wise.

Other visitors included Dame Nellie Melba, the celebrated opera singer. Accompanied by some friends, she sits on a set which appears to be the prop room from *Behind the Screen*. Syd produces the studio cat, and it is handed round to be admired. Vaudeville artist Bert Levy is shown around the set of *The Adventurer* by Chaplin, and the camera pans far enough to show the scaffold holding it up, and the painted backcloth.

Chaplin devoted care to these little visitor reels. In 1923, an English couple (Sir Albert and Lady Naylor-Leyland) are treated to a series of camera tricks – simple, stop motion shots with furniture and people appearing and disappearing.[14]

As intriguing as the visitors were, far more exciting were long-forgotten scenes from important films, like *Shoulder Arms*. When the first of these came up I failed to recognise it. Charlie leads three diminutive children along a street. The children are dressed like him. He stops the children, and disappears out of shot for a few moments; when he reappears, he is wiping his lips. It's a subtle joke for a period when much of the country was under wartime prohibition. An even subtler joke follows. Charlie arrives home, and no sooner has he stepped over the threshold than all hell breaks loose. He deposits the children outside and shuts the door. In Charlie's household, war has been declared. A shower of missiles hurtles towards him. The beauty of the sequence lies in the fact that Charlie's harridan wife is never shown. We simply see Charlie trying to reason with her, and dodging her unerring aim. No war could be worse than the domestic battleground. Charlie sets off to enlist.

We find Charlie sitting shyly on a bench. A soldier works at a desk in the foreground. A door is marked FRANCIS MAUD Examining Physician. Closer on Charlie; ordered to remove his clothes. He does so, without removing his hat or dropping his cane. But, in the interests of the censors, he retains his trousers. The soldier leaves. Charlie creeps to the door of the doctor's surgery. A shadow falls on the glass panel – ye gods, thinks Charlie, Francis Maud – it's a woman! It certainly looks like one. Charlie takes fright and pops into the next door office. There follows a delightful sequence like a scene from a Feydeau farce shot over the top of the interconnecting office walls. We see Charlie's head, a white blob in the background, as Edna, playing a secretary, walks up and down in her office. As she turns her head, Charlie vanishes. As she turns back, he pops back up. The scene might be puzzling to a modern audience. Had Charlie removed all his clothes, trousers included, his desperate anxiety to avoid females would ring true. But in the period of the Great War, men were considered ill-mannered to appear without their jackets, even in warm weather. Besides, the audience is supposed

---

14. A copy of this sequence is in the National Film Archive, donated by Sir Vivyan Naylor-Leyland.

to think he *has* removed all his clothes. Only the censor prevented him doing it more obviously. Dr Francis Maud (Albert Austin) comes out to look for him, and orders him into his surgery. Charlie obliges with a hilariously camp, mincing act which culminates in him bowing low, like an Egyptian slave in a Theda Bara film. Then begins a sequence which I would count among my favourite Chaplin moments. It is played in silhouette entirely on the glass panel of the door. Dr Maud shoves a spatula into Charlie's mouth. He taps his chest. The handle pops out and strikes Dr Maud, who pushes it back in. Another tap, and out it pops again. The next time it fails to do so. Dr Maud produces a pair of pincers, but clumsily drops them down Charlie's throat. He needs a fish-hook and a line to recover it. After some skilful angling, success! And Charlie coughs up the spatula as well. Shadowplay may be older than the theatre itself, but this sequence is pure cinema. And, simple as it is, I cannot work out precisely how it was done.

It must have broken Chaplin's heart to have been forced to cut these marvellous sequences. But distribution was ruled by the exhibitors and when Chaplin gave them a choice – a 5 reeler or a 3 reeler – they plumped for the shorter film. (You could make more money with a shorter film because you could run more performances.) Charlie's autobiography confirmed that these scenes were intended for *Shoulder Arms*, but he gives a different reason for discarding them. And he provides an ending to the scene in the office which was not included on the reel we saw (something was certainly missing).

> "*Shoulder Arms* was originally planned to be a five-reeler. The beginning was to be 'Home Life', the middle 'The War', and the end 'The Banqueting', showing all the crowned heads of Europe celebrating my heroic act of capturing the Kaiser. And, of course, in the end I wake up. The sequences before and after the war were discarded. The banquet was never photographed, but the beginning was. The comedy was by suggestion, showing Charlot walking home with his family of four children. He leaves them for a moment, then comes back wiping his mouth and belching. He enters the house and immediately a frying pan comes into the picture and hits him on the head. His wife is never seen, but an enormous che-

> mise is hanging on the kitchen line, suggesting her size. In the next sequence, Charlot is examined for induction and made to strip down to the altogether. On a bevelled glass office-door he sees the name 'Dr Frances' [sic]. A shadow appears to open the door, and, thinking it is a woman, he escapes through another door and finds himself in a maze of glass-partitioned offices where lady clerks are engrossed in their work. As one lady looks up, he dodges behind a desk, only to expose himself to another, eventually escaping through another door into more glass-partitioned offices, getting further and further away from his base, until he finds himself out on a balcony, nude, overlooking a busy thoroughfare below. This sequence, although photographed, was never used. I thought it better to keep Charlot a nondescript with no background and to discover him already in the army."[15]

As if this wasn't exciting enough, there followed a sequence extraordinary by any standards. It opened with a long shot of an old man in a battered top hat shambling down an alley, which might have come from a Cruikshank engraving (and probably did), and hobbling down the steps of a dosshouse. It is a shock to see Chaplin in different makeup, particularly one designed to make him look 60. It isn't a very convincing makeup – it is almost as grotesque as some of Campbell's – but Chaplin compensates for that by his performance. By the end of the sequence, no doubt remains that he is the eccentric old Professor Bosco, as it says on his box: FLEA CIRCUS. He has a twitch to his shoulder, and a sag to the knee. He pays the old Jew at the entrance (Underwood), and takes hold of his beard and moves it aside as though opening a door. He shambles past the sleeping down-and-outs to the empty bed, sits down and, after scratching a bit, opens his jacket and commands the fleas to return to their box. "It's *Limelight*," I cried. I remember being sick with laughter when I saw the flea circus sequence of *Limelight*, at the age of 14. But in *The Professor*, the gag is even more elaborate. He has the invisible flea jump through a hoop – by making a circle of finger and thumb. He suddenly catches sight of a tramp (Bergman) scratching.

---

15. C. Chaplin, *My Autobiography*, London, Max Reinhardt 1964, pp. 218 - 219.

(And by this time each one of us was scratching.) He opens the box and counts. One missing! He strides towards the beard, extracts the flea with delicacy, examines it – no, it isn't one of his. He replaces it. He flattens his opera hat, puts it under the pillow, and lies down. As he stretches out, his feet push the fleas' box on to the floor. Pause. A cut to long shot and all the other inmates begin to scratch. The Professor quickly takes in the extent of the disaster. He jumps up and produces a whip, a commanding figure. Slashing this way and that, he marshals all his fleas and whips them back into the box. Back to bed he goes, and relaxes. A mangy dog pads softly up to the box, pokes her head inside and (in the same take – thanks presumably to itching powder applied as the animal wanders offscreen for a moment) the poor dog begins to scratch its hindquarters. Then the Professor begins to scratch. It is brilliant the way Chaplin conveys that he is scratching himself because he hears scratching, not because he is itching. And when he realises there is no itch, he slowly straightens up, expecting the worst. He examines the box as the dog gallops away, and shrieks with alarm, as the awful thought hits him – the dog is disappearing with his entire circus! He sets out in pursuit and the sequence (and the film) ends in the Cruikshank alley, the Professor staggering after the dog as fast as his sagging knees will carry him. "Do you know," said Miss Ford, "I had never seen that before." "Why not?" I asked. "Charlie thought so little of it," said Miss Ford. "That's one of the best things I've ever seen him do," I said. My guess was that Chaplin shot this around 1919. He had played around with the dosshouse idea as early as 1915, when he made some scenes for his feature comedy *Life*, which he abandoned, but which Essanay cut into *Triple Trouble*, after Chaplin had left the company. It was an act which infuriated him, and many others, but exhibitors were glad of the money they made from it.

Chaplin returned to the dosshouse theme in *The Kid*, and he produced such a splendid sequence that I would imagine he had got the theme out of his system. There were many holdups on *The Kid*. Chaplin often found embarking on a different project both a relaxation and a stimulus. I suspect he started on *The Professor* around this period. We later came across some rushes from *The Professor*. They provided as many problems as clues. Chuck Riesner was on the film, but then he was with Chaplin, on and off, for most of the First National period. In a slightly different dosshouse set, although with the same old Jew as

The Chaplin studio on La Brea was one of the few allowed in Hollywood itself, and to suit the city fathers it was disguised as an 'English village'

caretaker, Charlie played a bellhop, in torn and ragged old uniform. His job is to give the inmates their early morning call.

One black man refuses to wake up. Charlie produces some dice and shakes them by the black man's ear. He responds instantly. This hangover from *The Cure* is puzzling; perhaps Chaplin intended to appear in his normal makeup to play the bellhop, while various characters of various sorts wandered in and out of the dosshouse.

But David Robinson discovered some cables at Vevey, among the Sydney Chaplin effects, which were dated 1923 and which referred to *The Professor* as a completed two-reeler.[16]

16. While we were examining documents at Vevey, we found an outline for *The Circus*: Suggestion for opening. THE TRAVELLER
    Under the archway of a bridge is a jungle of hobos. Some asleep some sitting around – one stirring food in a can over the fire. Charlie comes into the camp. He looks around fastidiously – takes out a handkerchief – dusts off a rock and sits down. One bum looks up and inquires – "What's your line?" Charlie answers "I am a circus man". Bum looks at him incredulously. He notices look and takes from under his arm a small box labelled "Flea Circus". Business ad lib with fleas. In putting fleas away for night, Charlie discovers one gone – goes over to bum with long beard – picks flea from beard, regards it and puts it back. It is evidently not one of circus. All asleep. In movements in sleep, flea circus is overturned and fleas escape. Scratching commences among bums but fleas concentrate on dog. Dog finally gets up in agony and whines, waking Charlie. He notices overturned flea circus – watches dog and jumps to the right conclusion. Pursuit of dog which goes into the lake, drowning circus.

Nothing could match *The Professor*, and for several rolls, nothing did. Take after take of orange and lemon groves showed Hollywood at its most pastoral. Puffs of smoke caused the studio to appear, stage by stage, in time-lapse photography. This was for *How to Make Movies*. Not only did the studio appear by magic, in a curious epilogue, the whole place disappeared by magic, too, leaving the countryside untouched and an angry property owner ordering Chaplin off his land. ("I never thought it would last," said Chaplin.) Wrapped up amongst all this was an odd sequence from the Essanay period. Chaplin looks incredibly young. He is seated at his desk, reading fan mail and sniffing the perfumed stationery. The butler enters, opens the safe and removes Chaplin's hat, boots and trousers.

Chaplin kept this scene (which was, strictly speaking, Essanay property) presumably because he knew one day it would be useful. And sure enough, he reshot it for *How to Make Movies*. In the new version, Chaplin reads the fan mail at his desk while Tom Harrington, the butler, walks to a concrete vault. "Where the valuables are stored" says a title. He emerges with Chaplin's boots.

8. The Circus

The climax to the mammoth viewing session was a pile of cans – 21,000 feet of uncut rushes for *The Circus*. Chaplin never used them in the final film, and the fact that they existed in their original form proved that he had never even cut them together. Miss Ford told us that when he reissued the film, in the 1960s, he realised it was rather short. She persuaded him to look at this material. He began to plough through it, and gave up. *The Circus* had been a miserable experience – probably the most traumatic of his career. The studio burned down, Lita Grey was divorcing him, and her lawyers insisted on a full revelation in open court of all her accusations. The yellow press – and the regular press – printed everything. When the lawyers moved to attach Chaplin's property, he decided to stop *The Circus* in mid-production. Begun in 1926, it was not completed until 1928.

Apart from a sequence showing Charlie calling for the girl (Merna) and waiting for her outside her caravan, all the rushes took place outside

The Circus (1928)

Rehearsals in *How to Make Movies*. Tom Wilson, Loyal Underwood, Chaplin, Henry Bergman, Jack Wilson, Edna Purviance

the circus. My theory as to why Chaplin did not use them is because he decided – or was persuaded – to keep the entire narrative, once it reached the circus, within the confines of the circus encampment.

To try to make sense of the jumble was tempting, but futile. A lot of it took place in a restaurant, and Charlie had a fight with a tough yegg which he sometimes won, and sometimes lost. The tough yegg – (the period term for safecracker) – appeared to have an identical twin, thanks to double-exposure. And one of these double exposures spent an unconscionable amount of time flicking lumps of sugar at Charlie.

Genius is said to be an infinite capacity for taking pains, and this material revealed Chaplin's genius to a painful degree. He retook everything, and it was often impossible to detect what he was trying to improve. A poster on the restaurant wall did not show up clearly enough, so it was replaced, and this meant that virtually the entire first part of the restaurant scene had to be reshot. There were so many takes of the yegg flipping sugar – thirty-five – that we gaped in open-mouthed astonishment, and cried, "Not another!" It substantiated all the stories one had heard; Chaplin used film heedlessly.

The intense hard work came across, too – it was intense hard work to plough through it all. And yet the frequent surprises and flourishes kept my enthusiasm high. Miss Ford and the others, however, had their stamina undermined by excessive retakes of the same thing. There was not quite the progression I'd hoped for. I could see Chaplin try a scene and improve it (slightly). But the improvement was so slight an ordinary audience would have needed animated graphs to appreciate it. Of course, part of the problem was that everything was in a muddle. The numbers were not consecutive, and one didn't know whether one was seeing the first attempt or the last.

Miss Ford was anxious that I should put the sequence together, and that it should eventually be put back into *The Circus*. "It was always rather short," she said. "Perhaps you could edit it, and we could see whether or not we should put it into the main film." She had in mind a kind of reconstruction job, similar to *Napoleon*, which might give the film a new lease of life. I was not averse to editing it – in fact I couldn't wait – although I did not think one should put into a film material rejected (for whatever reason) by the man who made it. But that was an ethical question which could wait until the job was done. "I'll try and cut it in Chaplin's style," I said. "He would have said that that was impossible," said Miss Ford, crushingly.

Now I had seen everything in the Chaplin vault, I was able to reassure David, when he returned from holiday, that we did indeed have a programme. The only drawback was that virtually none of our interviews applied to any of this material. There was nothing of *The Pilgrim* or *The Gold Rush*, and the one scene from *City Lights* did not include the blind girl! David wrote a letter to Rachel Ford: "I have just got back from my holiday and have been reading with very mixed feelings Kevin's notes on the two days you spent viewing at Denham. Mixed because whilst I'm delighted at the thought of so much treasure, I realise with envy the treat that I missed."[17]

He drafted the plans we had for the programme: The working title would be *The Unknown Chaplin*. Using film, stills and interviews, we would show a glimpse of Chaplin's creative process. Thanks to the miraculous fact that such fine examples of his rushes survive, we can follow the development of a gag, and can see it becoming more and more refined. We can sense the atmosphere on the set, as Chaplin and the others burst into laughter at the end of a scene. We can see his first attempts at routines which later became famous – the flea routine from *Limelight*, the barber-chair routine from *The Great Dictator* – and we can see ideas persisting through all the films. To make the comparisons, he pointed out, we would need to refer occasionally to a finished film, and this would involve the co-operation of Mo Rothman. As an inducement, Thames would consider giving him a percentage. And, obviously, there would be a percentage for the Chaplin family. "We can never express our gratitude strongly enough for the fact that you rescued this priceless material. Now that it exists, it would be an appalling thought if somehow we failed in finding a way of presenting the material that would both amaze and entertain and also illuminate our understanding of Chaplin's genius."

The letter contained no mention of Raymond Rohauer.

---

17. David Gill to Rachel Ford, 9 September 1980.

9. Luminous Excursions

David Stone, of the Gate Cinema, announced that *A Woman of Paris* in October would open the new Camden Plaza. I was asked by the Stones to interview Michael Powell, the famous British producer-director, for *Time Out*. Powell acknowledged that it was this film which turned him on to the cinema.

I had seen the film in a barely visible print from the Russian archive at the Library of Congress in Washington. (I took the precaution of arranging for a Russian interpreter, but when the film was put on the viewing table, it proved to have not Russian, but Serbo-Croatian subtitles!) So my reaction to the film had been one of mild interest. At last I was able to appreciate its brilliance. It was made with such wit, such understatement, it became, at once, my favourite Chaplin film. There was one serious drawback: the music track. Chaplin may have supervised it, but the music was simply wrong for the picture.

It was also recorded far too loud, presumably a result of Chaplin's deafness. The theatre was not full, and there was no feeling that the film would suddenly find the audience it had lacked on its original release. Nevertheless, a reception had been arranged for Oona, presided over by Mo Rothman. It was the first time David and I had set eyes on the dreaded Mo. He was well cast as a tycoon with a heart of stone so long as you knew the facts. In a conference, you would never pick him out from a hundred other middle-aged American businessmen. (He was, in fact, Canadian.) What set him apart on this occasion was that he had brought both his new wife and his ex-wife. His ex-wife, being Oriental, was an exotic feature of the party. Any hopes of talking to him were dashed by his elusive quality – we had an impression of him brushing the backs of our chairs as he sped from one bright spark to another.

That Sunday, my wife Virginia took a call from Miss Ford and left me the message: "She said Oona had tried to talk to 'The Bandit' about your project, but he paid no attention and only talked of a musical. But Miss Ford overheard him telling her you planned to meet."

Sadly, *A Woman of Paris* was a flop, and it came off after a short run, despite some excellent reviews.

Meanwhile, I flew to Los Angeles for a film historians' convention. I was only there for a weekend, but I managed to attend an illustrated lecture by Jackie Coogan at California Institute of Technology, and I spoke on the phone to Clyde Cook, who had been in the Karno outfit with Chaplin. I also met Miles Kreuger, of the Institute of the American Musical, who had in his collection a rare record of Chaplin conducting the Abe Lyman orchestra in 1923. While I was away, David met lawyers and formulated what seemed a reasonable offer to Mo Rothman: £7,500 on the signing of the contract for a maximum of ten minutes. Any additional footage would be paid pro rata on first transmission. He also presented an offer to Roy Export – i.e. Chaplin – of 20% of the net profits.

At this stage, we were thinking of a single programme, a fact Miss Ford often referred to. She considered we had enough for one programme, and so did we, although our idea of the length varied. It might be 52 minutes, it might be 75.

But at this point, the possibility of any programme was in doubt. Mo Rothman rejected Thames's offer, saying, "£7,500 guaranteed up front is nothing". He wanted a share in the distribution profits. He accepted that his share would be less than Roy Export's, but, he emphasised, Oona would feast, Thames would feast, he didn't want "just crumbs from the Royal table". On the other hand, he was aware of Lady Chaplin's enthusiasm for the project, and did not want to be responsible for blocking it. Thames adjusted their offer to Roy; it became 50% of net profits of distribution outside the UK. The Mo Rothman saga continued...

The first person we filmed for the programme was Ivor Montagu, an old friend of Chaplin's, and a man who deserved a programme in his own right. In the normal course of events, Ivor Montagu would be a Peer of the Realm, ensconced in the House of Lords. As a young man, however, he became a communist, and an avowed disciple of the Soviet Union. He joined the British film industry and ran an editing and titling company. Through his connection with the Film Society he got to know Eisenstein, and in the late twenties accompanied him on a trip to Hollywood, where he met Chaplin for the first time. Montagu was extremely fat, extremely amusing, and he behaved in a fashion altogether opposed to the stereotyped Stalinist hard-liner. Mrs Montagu ("Hell" – her name was Eileen Hellstern) was alarmed by the number of the crew that flooded into their little mock-Tudor bungalow in Garston, Herts. But while I was apologising, I suddenly realised that it was partly

Ivor's fault. As a strong union man, he had supported the crewing requirements that we found so onerous (ten to shoot an interview you could easily do with two). Montagu barely touched upon politics – he was more concerned with tennis.

Ivor Montagu

It wasn't until I went out to Hollywood in 1929 that I met Charlie. Of course, one of my ideals was to meet him. I knew both (G. Bernard) Shaw and (H.G.) Wells and among the introductions I collected were two from them, and as soon as I got out to Hollywood I took them along to Charlie's studio and there met (Alf) Reeves, studio manager. I recognised from the voice that he came from just the part of Brixton that my wife was born in, and I brought in Camberwell and Denmark Hill to the conversation, and this made us such bosom pals that he said he would pass (the introductions) directly to Charlie. No doubt I would be seeing him immediately, but this didn't happen. I called every few weeks, and Mr Reeves began to grow embarrassed and he said, "The trouble is, Mr Chaplin is trying to think out what he will do for you because he wants to think up something special." And in the end he grew compassionate and said, "Look here, I'll take you inside the studio and then I'll say, 'Here's Mr Chaplin' and you'll meet him." I said that wouldn't do so I hung on and finally got a telephone call from Kono, the butler who did everything for him in a social way. Would I come round next day Saturday to a tennis party? I afterwards heard from Georgia [Hale] that it was one of those he gave every now and then to try and kill off the various people to whom he owed an invitation.

Charlie was a very good tennis player. He seemed to be able to attain any skill he wanted – one sees that kind of thing from time to time in the films. Take, for example, *The Gold Rush*. That dance with the rolls is in itself a marvellous feat of dexterity that he taught himself. I mean he had coaches and things, but it was his will power that made him reach the standard at tennis that he attained. He used to have a friendly rivalry with Douglas Fairbanks, because anything that Douglas did – running, the athletic line, playing tennis – Charlie immediately took up and played it until he could do it better than Douglas. It was only when Douglas took to golf that Charlie said he wouldn't follow him.

Something like hairdressing, which after all is a great skill, he certainly didn't acquire merely for *The Great Dictator*. When we went to stay with him, as we did on our last weekend in Hollywood, he gave my wife the most marvellous haircut she's ever had. He certainly mastered any skills that he set out to master.

Charlie had an absolutely insatiable curiosity. In this he corresponded to many other people I've met, eminent

Douglas Fairbanks and Chaplin during the making of *A Modern Musketeer* (1917)

in their field – science, art, writing whatever it may be. The one thing in common with them is an avidity to know everything they possibly can about anything, in case it may come in useful to them in their field. Charlie was that sort of creative artist. When he met people he was the observer as well as the actor. Afterwards he would not make fun of them, but he would describe everything and you can see perfectly clearly what he got out of it. I'm quite sure that every new experience, every society lion that wanted to visit him, was somebody who was added to the gallery.

On Christmas Day, after a good deal of tennis and an English lunch, he said, "Let me tell you about *City Lights*." We were sitting in armchairs in his drawing room and he acted the whole of *City Lights* to us. Now, the trouble was for me that this sort of thing was a one-off experience in one's life. One wanted never to forget it. It was a privilege, not to have been dreamed of when one came to Hollywood. But I'd been playing tennis hard, and I'd had a good meal, and what with the warmth and everything, I could not stay awake. This was one of the most embarrassing situations that it was possible to be in. My wife was sitting near enough to dig me metaphorically with a pin. But that's how I first became acquainted with *City Lights*. I think I got from that incident really what I look on as the most blinding illumination about Charlie's work. For me it has been the key to understanding it all, and why it is good, why it excels that of so many other film comedians. It was quite clear from the way he was talking and the way he was telling the story that he was not identifying with the Chaplin figure at all. He was calling it "the tramp" all the time, speaking of it in the third person, and he was the director who invented these things that were happening, who did these things with that figure there. He did them with a certain kind of relish in the misfortunes he was inflicting on him, and there may have been some pride in the way he got out of them. Nonetheless, he was the doer of those sufferings, rather than the sufferer. The point with him is that he was a creator; he told the story, invented the characters, what happened to them was born out of his experience – the sorrows, the emotions they aroused – these were all planned by him. He showed for the first time the degree of emotion the film was capable of inspiring in the audience. This was done not just by the actor but by the planner, and that's what Charlie was in his work. A few days later he asked us round to see a rough cut. I had a feeling that by not having somebody to bully him, and a schedule to keep to, he risked being too near his subject in the end to judge it. I think he was sometimes too long with his subject. He wanted to make them perfect – nothing but perfection would be right. But I think with comedy you can lose judgement at just the moment at which it ceases to be funny, or at which, if it went on, it would be a little funnier.

For example, that scene in *City Lights* in which he's looking in a shop window and he keeps stepping back to get a different view (trying not to look at the nude statue) and behind him there's a hole in the pavement for a lift. That gap – it looks every moment as if he's going to step back into it. The climax of the comedy is that he never does. As I remember it, when we first saw it longer, he took the comedy to hysteria. When one saw the finished cut, it was just not long enough to reach that point.

When *City Lights* was nearly finished, he began to grow very nervous and have huge ups and downs. Sometimes he would say that it was the greatest picture ever made. At others, he would talk about how the picture was going to be a complete failure, nobody was going to see it, he would be ruined. Georgia digs him in the ribs and says "Go on, Charlie, you'll have a million dollars left". "What is a million dollars? What is a million dollars?" If one hadn't known Chaplin it would have sounded an affectation, but not at all. It was really the essence of him. He had reached a position where he could make a picture exactly as he liked and spend as long as he liked making it. That would cost a million dollars. He had about two million. Now, all right, he would have had a million dollars left, but that would have meant that he'd completely lost that freedom. He would no longer have been free to make a picture as he wanted. It would be back to the grindstone with a schedule and a budget and everything else.

A very odd thing happened one night. We played a very cruel game that was current – in this game one of those present, chosen by lot, has to go outside the room. Those inside, equipped with pieces of paper with qualities written down, such as charm, sense of humour, beauty – each quality is discussed in respect of the absent friend as to how many marks out of ten he warrants for that particular quality. And the victim outside has to mark his own paper, come back into the room and undergo the ordeal, reading out his own estimation of himself and hearing the estimate of the company. Well, this game was duly played, and I hope it will never be played again anywhere, and the trouble was that when Charlie read his, when it came to sense of humour he had modestly given himself nine, but the assembled company had given him four. Now, was this a joke we were playing on Charlie? Not at all. It was quite a learned and philosophic discussion about the meaning of sense of humour. For sense of comedy we would have had to give him perhaps eleven out of ten. But humour suggests a certain detachment and an ability to see the funny side of what happens to oneself, and this Charlie was much too shy ever to feel. I don't think he liked to look into himself and judge himself. It wasn't that he was afraid of other people, or ashamed of other people, but he himself wouldn't have liked it and so that was a characteristic.

He was asked from time to time whether he was Jewish and he would never answer for publication because he said that for anybody to say they were not Jewish implied that they didn't wish to be thought Jewish. His story was that he had Spanish gipsy (blood) through his mother and that he got his curly hair that way.

> I was in Berlin in the early days of the Nazis and I happened to see a book called *Jews Are Looking At You*.[18] It showed all kinds of people, many of them not Jews at all, and among them I found Charlie. The caption under the picture read: "This boring and talentless acrobatic Jew shown in the cinemas of the world to the discomfiture of the viewers, etc. etc." I thought he ought to have a look at this and I sent him a copy. Now in all the years I knew Charlie, he often sent me Christmas cards, telegrams, telephone calls but he only sent me one letter – and it was a short letter thanking me for that book. I always think that it may well have contributed to his resolve to make *The Great Dictator*.

A plaque to mark the fact that Chaplin lived at 287 Kennington Road was to be unveiled on 19 December 1980 (He had actually lived next door). We went early; a crowd had already gathered and a band was blasting out such inappropriate tunes as the James Bond theme and *Jesus Christ Superstar*. Ralph Richardson gave a speech, and so did a man from the Church of England Children's Society – a reminder of Chaplin's youth. I noticed Rachel in deep conversation with Mo Rothman, and in the pub afterwards she announced she had broken through. At last we could be certain of access to extracts from the Chaplin films.

Another great event; in February, 1981, Rohauer announced that he had finally worked out a way of getting his material out of France.

---

18. One of a series popular in pre-Nazi Germany with titles like *Children Are Looking At You, Animals Are Looking At You.*

10. Vault Farce

Rohauer admitted that he had a lot of other material, apart from the Chaplin footage, stored in vaults in France. He suggested bringing it all over. "Then you'll have the Chaplin material here, wouldn't you?" "Yes," thought David. "We'd also have a lot of stuff we weren't interested in." But the ends justified any means.

Now Rohauer wanted David to arrange trips to Paris for him. We all nodded sagely. "He's just stringing you along for free flights to France." "Maybe," said David. "We've got to take the risk."

Rohauer's channel-hopping went on for four months. Things we all hoped would happen didn't. The person he was to meet wasn't there, or was sick, or the car broke down. Alibis that fitted our scenario of suspicion. But David was more than tenacious; he was relentless. Long after ordinary mortals would have given up in disgust he continued to meet Rohauer, to accept his excuses, to advance him money and to put up with his midnight telephone calls. Above all, he treated him like a friend, and I'm sure it was this quality that kept Rohauer going. For the experience must have been humiliating – knowing the material was there, but being sabotaged by those who were supposed to be safeguarding it.

On one occasion, when we all thought we were on the brink of D-Day, David hired a van to meet Rohauer near Lyons. The van got hopelessly lost, Rohauer had to leave for Paris, and the van's owner, Freight Bond, billed us for three times the agreed amount. One morning, David and editor Trevor Waite set off at crack of dawn to meet a vehicle coming off the boat at Newhaven. I was frustrated to be left out of this adventure, but Rohauer's instructions were clear; at almost every meeting, he had raised the matter of the *Sunday Times* article, which he was convinced I had written under John Baxter's name. When the boat docked, the vehicle was delayed by customs. David and Trevor sat for four hours. "My apprehension and distrust were at their height," said David. "And then I met the driver. He had one eye, which never really looked at you. He was a parody of Robert Newton as Long John Silver. 'You should have been with me the last few days,' he chortled. 'I've seen things. I've been to garages and barns and chateaux. I don't know what you'll make of it all. They're all rusty cans. Hundreds of 'em. Look at my hands. Can't get it off.' He warned David not to try to rush the customs, otherwise they would make trouble. As it happened, the customs were within their rights to make a fuss on this occasion because the truck contained enough nitrate to blow the customs sheds out of Newhaven Harbour. Highly inflammable in its normal state, nitrate becomes more dangerous as it decomposes. And one could safely assume a lot of this material was in an unstable condition.[19] "Ours was the last van to go through," said David. "The back was unlocked and wound up and there was pile upon pile of cans, of varying degrees of rust, spreading to the far back of this enormous van. They had started about ten high, but had been knocked about en route. The van was a mosaic of ancient film cans. The customs man groaned. 'Jesus Christ,' he said. 'What are we going to do with all this?' He looked at the list and then clambered up and tried to identify the titles. He wasn't going to release us until he had identified every title on his inventory. The idea of nitrate hadn't occurred to him. We negotiated that if we could find ten titles on the list, that would be enough. He was clearly beginning to lose interest. A crowd had gathered round the van, saying, 'Blue movies then, is it?' We found those ten titles, he ticked off his list with relief and cleared us through. But we still had this problem with the one-eyed driver. Was he going to disappear with the precious cans? He was. 'My instructions are that Mr Rohauer will meet us at the vaults tomorrow. So I'll take the van to the yard – it's a lockup, so it'll be all right.' I thought: That's a good one. Should we follow him? But I said, 'Fine. Here's the address of the vaults.'

"To avoid another night of tension, I rang Rohauer and he confirmed the story. In fact, looking back, everything was absolutely straight and above-board – as far as it could be in such a cloak-and-dagger operation. All the little hitches had been genuine hitches."

---

19. The danger has been exaggerated. David kept a roll of unstable nitrate on an old bonfire in his garden throughout a summer, and nothing happened. Nitrate is as dangerous as the petrol in your car.

11. Evidence of our Eyes

It was a miserably cold February morning when the huge vehicle drove up to the vaults at Perivale, to be met by David, Trevor and Raymond Rohauer. An assistant from Thames, Malcolm Newnam, had been pressganged into helping, too. David got him to take a souvenir photograph of them all, lined up in front of the cans, frozen but proud.

"Only then did it really begin to hit me," said David. "We were sorting out the cans and we had decided that all the Chaplins would go in one vault, and all the rest into another. There were piles and piles of cans – thirty, forty, fifty cans just labelled *The Immigrant*... twenty, thirty, forty cans *Behind the Screen*... thirty, forty, fifty, sixty cans *The Cure*. And then, oh, we've only got six cans of *The Vagabond*. Tragic! We were soon in the kind of state where anything less than thirty or forty cans for one title was a major disappointment. I thought to myself, "Wait till Kevin hears about this!" He had said "Look inside the cans," and that was the next thing. They were very rusty, of course, and it was hard to get them open with freezing hands. But it was amazing – it was all nitrate negative – not positive, but negative, most of it in perfect condition, just as it had come out of the camera sixty-four years ago. I think Raymond was as surprised, and relieved, as we were. Some of it had gone – there was practically nothing of *Easy Street* or *The Vagabond*. But most of it was as good as the day it was born.

"A lot of the film was not Chaplin. Raymond was able to say, 'That is – that's not.' Then there was the enormous task of organising it all. How do you go about collating it? How can there be fifty cans of *The Immigrant*? What could be in those cans? Our next task was to view the material." David arranged with Colour Film Services – a nearby laboratory – to hire us some space at their Perivale plant, and we shipped in our Steenbeck. This viewing machine, made in Germany, was fitted with special shrunken sprockets to enable it to accept ancient nitrate.

On the morning of 12 February 1981, a hire car picked me up from Belsize Park and drove me to the Mayfair Hotel, where I met Raymond Rohauer. For two people who had been at each others' throats for so many years, we survived the journey to Perivale in surprisingly agreeable spirits.

When we reached the laboratory, we discovered that no one was expecting us. There was no sign of David or Trevor, so Raymond began to have the uneasy feeling we had come to the wrong place. I fired "Thames Television" at everyone in sight, but no glimmer of recognition from anyone. It is strange how often this happens; you make arrangements for an important event, and somehow you imagine the people at the other end of the phone are infected with the same degree of enthusiasm. It is deflating – and, I suppose, salutary – to discover that they have no interest either in your project or in you.

Raymond and I sat in the canteen sipping tea, waiting for David and Trevor. It was such a red letter day, I could not imagine them wanting to miss a minute of it. But they were quite incredibly late, due to severe traffic jams. Rohauer and I discussed the Chaplin material, how he

Victory! Raymond Rohauer, David Gill and the pantechnicon

After a preview of *Unknown Chaplin* at Thames TV, David Gill, Oona Chaplin, Rachel Ford, Kevin Brownlow, Geraldine Chaplin

found it and whether the story could ever be told. Our viewing area was a bleak corner, at the end of a corridor of offices. The Steenbeck had been trundled in, and connected up, and all seemed ready. Eventually, David and Trevor turned up, with assistant editor Malcolm Newnam, who brought in a pile of cans. We eagerly clustered around the machine, as Trevor laced it up, and very gently eased the Steenbeck forward. The first can we chose because it was marked "Camera test" – was this the Lita Grey screen test which Rohauer had promised? It was in perfect condition, but it was not Lita Grey – it was Georgia Hale doing the final scene for *City Lights*. The film appeared on the ground-glass viewing screen and – although we all knew it was negative, we somehow expected a positive image to leap before our eyes. It was bewildering to see black where there should be whites, and whites where there should be black. Watching negative requires an adjustment of the eyes. Before we were able to achieve this, a smell hit our nostrils – a powerful and alarming smell – the smell of hypo. This is a stage in the decomposition of nitrate, which is a complex mixture. We could hear the first hypo section coming – a sticky sound, as though we were slowly unwinding a roll of Sellotape.

Just as the picture began to make sense to our untrained eyes, and we began to thrill to the first proof of our discovery, unsightly blobs appeared, like the onset of migraine. The picture was soon bombarded by these blobs, to the accompaniment of the violent sticky noise, until it was overwhelmed, and the only visible evidence were dancing shapes, the sort of thing Norman MacLaren used to do in his cartoons. The spacing inserted between the takes seemed mainly responsible – it was probably cheap stock which deteriorated before the rest, but took some of it with it. One could also see evidence of an interaction between the metal can and the celluloid. On a badly hypoed shot the film would jam in the gate and a pile of brown dust spread everywhere. But what amazed us was how little decomposition had taken place and how smoothly the 65-year-old negative went through.

Obviously the rolls had been hurriedly assembled after the main film had been negative-cut, because some of the shots were upside down. Trims were joined up together as a kaleidoscope of flashes. There was no order. Slowly each scene from each classic comedy became grindingly familiar, as Chaplin shot it again and again. A new scene would start, to be replaced by yet another take of the previous one. Slate boards appeared – but without any indication as to the number of takes. Usually, a slate board would be marked with the scene number and the take number: Scene 20 take 3. But Chaplin, not wishing to know how many times he had taken a scene, preferred to change the scene number, and ignore the take number. Thus we saw slates ranging from 1 to 779. "I once worried about the waste of film all these repetitions made," said Chaplin, "but now large figures don't mean anything to me."

The takes were often so similar we could see no difference, and we decided that this was due to the fact that two cameras were in use, one cranked by Rollie Totheroh, the other by Jack Wilson. Later on, we revised that opinion – the takes were uncannily alike but there seemed to be slight and subtle differences.

The first cans we looked at were from *The Adventurer* – Chaplin's last for Mutual, 1917. One sequence established a Spanish dancer, entertaining house guests at a grand party. Charlie has rescued Edna and her mother from drowning, and Edna has brought him back to the mansion, not knowing that he is an escaped convict. The Spanish dancer hurls herself round the room in wild abandon, shocking the other guests, but delighting Charlie. The more exotic her dance, the hotter he becomes. He undoes his tie, opens his collar, takes off his jacket – all strictly *de trop* at a smart function in 1917. Edna, seated beside him, is more shocked by him than by the dancer. Chaplin ran into trouble on this scene, for he was trying to flirt with two women here, and it was frustrating to watch how the scene flickered out. His interplay with the dancer, winking and giving her the eye, was delightful, but he abandoned it swiftly, and concentrated on the comic aspect of a man disrobing at a society function. His fever was apparently brought on by the dancer, and he knew the censors would have their scissors ready, so he had planned a joke to defuse the scene; he discovers he is sitting over a radiator, leaking steam. Poor Chaplin, we thought, as we watched thirty to sixty takes. But when we saw the final film, later, there was no sign of the radiator gag, or the Spanish dancer. Chaplin knew he had failed, and he was able to throw the whole sequence out. As filmmakers, we envied him the ability to spend so much time and so much film on a thorough exploration of an idea. And the freedom to discard it if it failed to work.

One surprise was Chaplin's total concentration on the performance to the exclusion of all else. Many filmmakers would take advantage of a retake to alter the camera setup. Not Chaplin. Once the camera was set, he never altered it. And the setup was always satisfactory, from the point of view of composition, and what it was intended to show. Directors can have sleepless nights wondering where to put the camera; for Chaplin it was a minor concern. I remember seeing him on the set of *Countess from Hong Kong* in the 'sixties, turning to the cameraman and indicating the shot he wanted by crossing his chest with his arm. He probably did exactly the same in 1917. Chaplin's direction was simple and clear, but always highly professional. I don't like to use that word in this context, but Chaplin has been criticised for his "old fashioned" direction for so long that it needs to be made clear that he knew his craft. He knew how to cover a scene, and he provided the elements of mid-shot and closeup whenever necessary. But he often left them out in the editing. His was the "proscenium arch" approach; he remained a man of the theatre, and his primary concern was to convey to the audience the action and emotion through the performances.

Sometimes he would get stuck on a scene of bewildering simplicity, and he would reshoot it dozens of times, until we all groaned, "not again!" The recognition scene in *The Adventurer* was just such a scene. Edna's father (Henry Bergman) is a judge, and when he is introduced to Charlie at the party he recognises him from when he stood before him in the dock. What Chaplin wanted from Bergman that he wasn't giving him is impossible to surmise; he plays every take exactly the same way.

There was a temptation to drop one's eyes, if only to rest them – for staring at the negative was quite a strain. But one daren't. There might have been a flash of something extraordinary between the slate boards, or even behind them. One of the most exciting discoveries was a shot of Chaplin pacing up and down, working out a gag with his closest associates, Albert Austin and Henry Bergman. Totheroh and Wilson must have wanted a quick test, for both cameras filmed it. One thing was apparent from the rushes. Chaplin might have regarded film as the cheapest commodity in his budget. But only when it was filming a scene. The moment the scene was over, and he had said "cut", Totheroh and Wilson had to stop cranking. It was surprising – and dismaying – that so few intimate moments passed the censorship of the crank. Yet right in the middle of *The Adventurer* appeared a long take of Chaplin conducting a visitor, vaudevillian Bert Levy, around the set. And there were many scenes which went wrong – such as a shot of the heavy, Eric Campbell, being placed on a stretcher. He has refused to rescue Edna or her mother, and when pitched into the water accidentally has tried to drown Chaplin. So Charlie picks the stretcher up by one end only; Campbell is supposed to slide off the other end into the water again. But he doesn't slide far enough. Or his fat stomach jams in the rail of the pier. The scene went wrong at least three times. Chaplin ended many takes with a grin at the camera – a smile of such sweetness and good humour that it suggested that the work may have been more enjoyable than it looked. The bombardment of takes meant that he and the players had to do their falls again and again. How Bergman or Austin put up with being battered by surf or banged against rocks so often is hard to imagine. Once, Chaplin falls backwards over a small rock with more energy than he intended, and a grip runs in to help him.

In each film, there was usually only one major sequence left out of the final film – an indication of how well Chaplin could sense the requirements of a two-reeler. Members of his stock company play many different parts in the same film – Henry Bergman was a prison guard, a pipe-smoking swimmer who also appears on the pier and the judge who remembers the convict. Campbell, on the other hand, is too obvious to play anything but his usual grotesque heavy. Campbell, incidentally, was a Scotsman who had specialised in Gilbert and Sullivan.[20] Albert Austin – an Englishman from Birmingham who had been with the Fred Karno troupe – played a guard and a butler.

Now that we had embarked wholeheartedly on *Unknown Chaplin*, I urged David to agree to go to America as soon as possible to film the interviews. He thought we should delay until we knew exactly what material we had, so we could ask the right questions. I agreed that that was the most sensible approach, but we might wait too long and the thought of losing Virginia Cherrill or Georgia Hale appalled me. There was no answer to this. David began to put the machinery of Thames into action. In between his phone calls, we ploughed on through roll after roll. The amazement of discovery gave way to a bland acceptance – "Oh no, no more cans of *The Adventurer*!" We had also begun to suspect that the vast majority of *The Adventurer* material consisted of scenes that were in the film. That was why we were so excited by the Spanish dancer and radiator scenes – they were unknown, fresh and revealing. But there was very little else that fitted those categories, and growing in our minds was the thought that perhaps all the material would simply be repeats of what we already knew.

We completed *The Adventurer* and turned to *The Cure*. And before we began, we looked at a 16mm print. *The Cure* had always been among my favourite Chaplins. Set in a health spa, it shows the misadventures of an advanced alcoholic. He turns up with a huge steamer trunk, packed with booze. My favourite moments when I saw the film as a child were those in which Charlie outwits the brutal masseurs. Chaplin abandoned his tramp outfit for this film, although he wore his moustache and carried his cane.

---

20. Kevin Macdonald's film about Campbell, *Chaplin's Goliath*, casts doubt on this Gilbert and Sullivan experience.

The first thing we noticed about the negative of *The Cure* was how well it went through the machine. The condition was almost perfect, and the celluloid amazingly supple. Our morale was boosted further by the first shot we saw. If you didn't know the film, it would be extremely puzzling – a pair of legs apparently sticking out of a manhole. Throughout the story, Charlie has sustained a vicious duel with Eric Campbell, he of the ghastly whiskers and tall hat. Eric has fierce gout and his foot, swathed in bandages, acts as a magnet for Charlie, who constantly falls over it, causing Campbell to rise from his bathchair in agony. It is sadistic and hilarious, and it is climaxed when Charlie, spinning out from a revolving door, collides with Albert Austin, who happens to be pushing Campbell in his bathchair. Austin and the bathchair hurtle down the steps towards the medicinal well, into which Campbell is propelled with a graceful dive. I say Campbell, but this first shot proved that it wasn't. The legs thrash about for a few moments, and then some men rush in and haul the poor fellow out – dripping and gasping and much slimmer and younger than Campbell. We ran the shot several times and David noticed something odd: "Do you see how he signals when he's had enough?" We looked closely and saw that he placed his legs together and was instantly rescued. The "medicinal well" was convincing enough at first sight, but on close examination it was nothing more than a canvas bag filled with water. There was a midshot of this, and because Chaplin was too far away to call "cut" (he was still spinning in the revolving door), Totheroh kept cranking. And one of the rescuers was easily recognisable as Eric Campbell.

As usual, the material was hopelessly jumbled – slate 23 followed by 160 followed by 405 – but suddenly we saw what might have been the original ending. Surviving prints of *The Cure* end with an abrupt and puzzling fadeout as Charlie and Edna conclude a romantic interlude by the well, and step forward. The shot we saw proves that Chaplin planned a final gag – as he steps forward, he disappears into the well. He then bounces up and down in the water, his arms thrust forward in a gesture of love, while Edna roars with laughter. It looked as though Chaplin was playing the fool for Edna's benefit,[21] but the scene is intact in some versions of *The Cure*. Slate 605 was an unusually well-lit shot of Charlie playing the piano; Edna, in some scene which was either lost

---

21. This ending has always been in *complete* prints (Bo Berglund).

or never shot, has given him a rose, and he lays it on the piano, and starts to play a soulful melody. He picks it up and realises it is artificial, which causes him to go berserk on the keyboard. But the most revealing, and exciting, slates showed Charlie in a totally different costume to the one he wears in the picture. These slates had early numbers, and it was obvious from those that Chaplin had begun *The Cure* playing not the drunk, but a bellhop. Having created the best-known costume of the twentieth century, the tramp, it is odd how often Chaplin rejected it. At Mutual he appeared as a policeman, a fireman, a convict. He spends most of *The Adventurer* in evening clothes. At Sennett, he played one picture without makeup or costume (*Tango Tangles*). And he began *The Cure* as a member of the staff, in uniform. The uniform gave rise to one marvellous gag: the lobby becomes jammed with inmates in their bathchairs and Charlie assumes the role of traffic cop to sort them all out.[22] But otherwise, Chaplin seemed to lose impetus. He stages a scene in the lobby in which he pushes a man in a bathchair. A lady passes the chair and pulls up her skirt to avoid contact with it. The sight of her ankles diverts Charlie's attention, and he runs the chair into Campbell's gouty foot. Campbell leaps from his seat, raising his hands in anguish. Charlie imagines he's pointing at something and stares at the roof. Campbell collapses, and Charlie whisks a handkerchief over the front of the chair, in case it's sustained damage. Campbell uses his good foot to kick him in the rear, sending him and the chair hurtling across the lobby floor, picking up a stout lady en route. Gasping with shock, she climbs off the patient's lap and Charlie indicates, "Only one passenger, please," before trundling out.

    This scene caused Chaplin a creative block. He repeated it a dozen times without being able to improve it. Chaplin often tried retaking a scene in the hope that he would be inspired to find a way of continuing it. But not this time. The adrenalin may have been flowing, but the ideas were not.

    David pointed out the drawback to the bellboy character when we saw the traffic cop scene: "He's on the side of authority," he said, "and he's bringing order out of chaos. That conflicts with the tramp character, who creates anarchy wherever he goes." The same thought must have occurred to Chaplin. He switched his attention to the exterior of the spa.

22. Harold Lloyd repeated this gag.

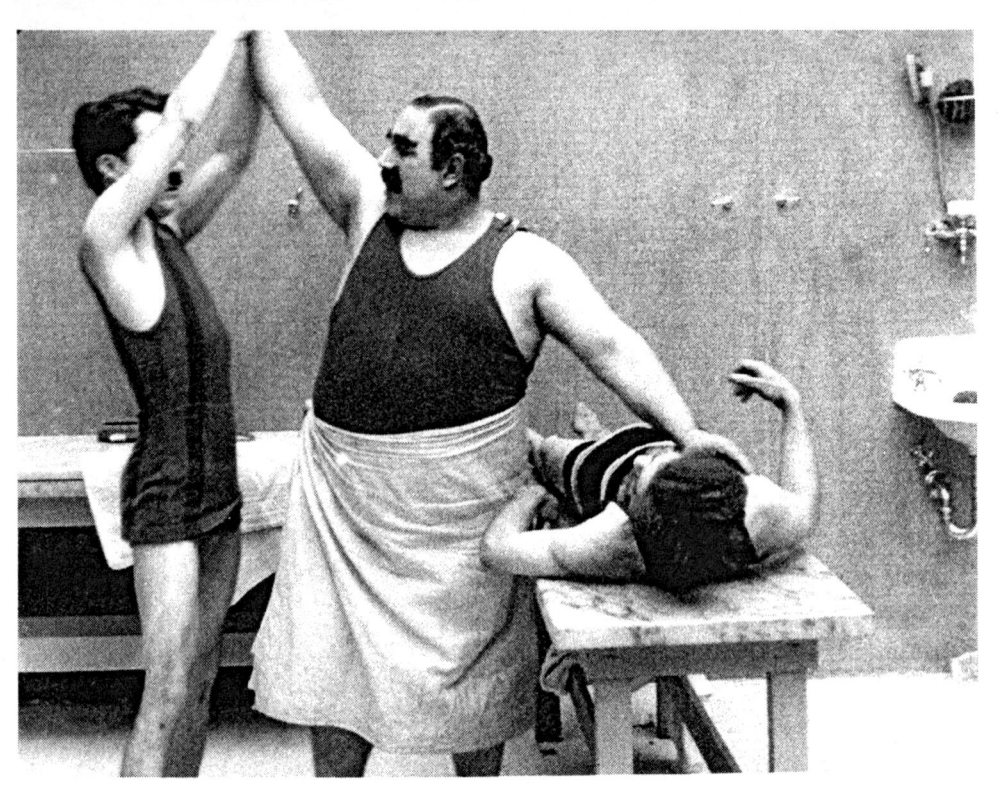

(Top) Henry Bergman as the masseur in *The Cure* (1917)
(Others) Chaplin's parody of the Tableaux, a risqué music hall routine in which beautiful girls posed in just this style

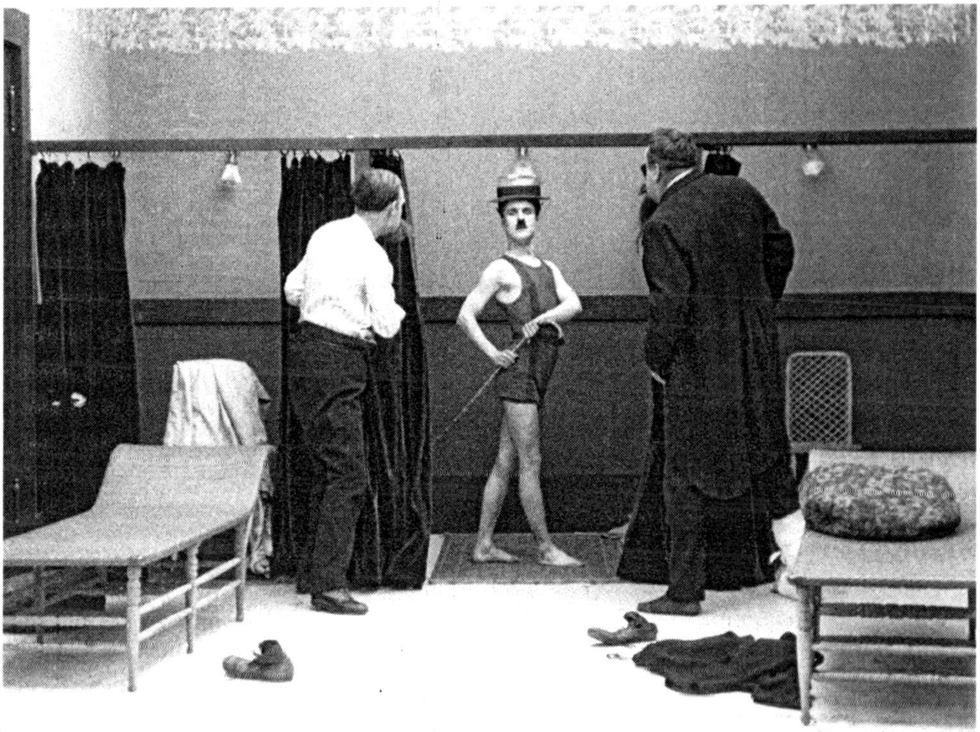

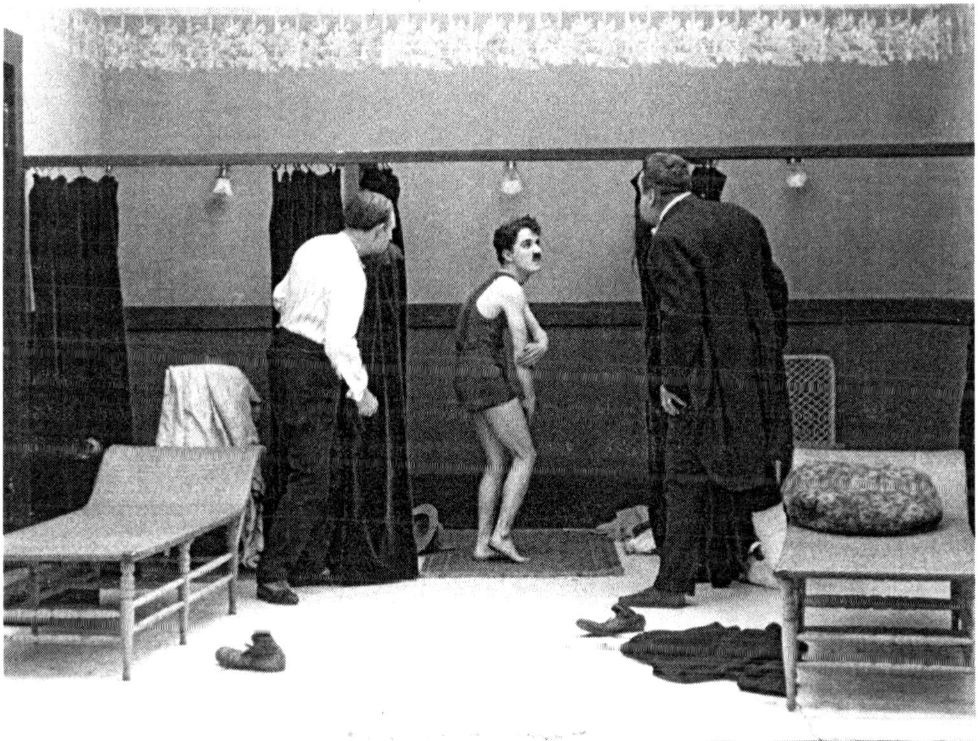

Slate 1 had established the place as a refuge for the middle-aged, its focal point a simple drinking fountain. Now he changed the drinking fountain to a medicinal well, and grouped his genteel patients around it. And out of the revolving door lurched John Rand, playing a drunk.

Chaplin won fame at Karno playing drunks. He directed by example; he showed his actors how to play their parts by playing those parts himself. One can imagine him showing John Rand how to do a drunk, winning laughs from the crew, and asking himself, "Why am I not doing this myself?"

Slate 84 was dramatic enough to cause us to cry out with surprise, for it showed that Chaplin and Rand had exchanged roles – Chaplin was now the drunk and Rand the bellhop. The only reminder of all he had discarded was a wheelchair. Charlie steps over it as he makes his way unsteadily towards the entrance of the spa.

By contrast to all this was another enormous haul of rare Chaplin material, in which we had very little interest. It, too, consisted of rushes and outtakes, all in excellent condition – but it belonged to the films of Syd Chaplin, Charlie's half-brother.

Syd had been by far the more famous comedian in England. Karno was so possessive of his talents that he wouldn't allow him to go to America, and sent his brother Charles instead. When Charles left Keystone, Mack Sennett replaced him with Sydney.[23] He made a successful three-reeler feature called *The Submarine Pirate*, and a number of short comedies, but he soon joined his brother as business manager. From the evidence of the rushes of films like *The Pawnshop*, he helped out on the direction too. Inevitably, Sydney was invited to make his own independent comedies, in the hope that he might repeat his brother's success. And some of them were popular. But I have never seen a Sydney Chaplin film to compare with the best of a Charlie Chaplin.

We took a look at a few rolls and, while their production values and lighting were superior, the humour was not. Sydney was sharper, more abrasive on the screen. He was a kind of precursor of the spiv of the 1940s. One did not warm to him.

---

23. A move that must have made sense to Sennett: Now I'll get the one who was a big star.

12. Light Blue Touchpaper...

Raymond Rohauer stayed with us for only a day, before he had to return to New York. We had to have the key to the vault, and we couldn't work without it, but the fact is astonishing enough to record: he left it with us. We were now in sole charge of all his Chaplin material. He also left us with the confident assurance that there was more to come. The next consignment from France would include out-takes from the majority of the other Chaplin films, right up to *Limelight*. All of which changed the dimension of our project. It also threatened our relationship with Rachel Ford. We had no doubt whatever that she regarded Rohauer as her arch enemy. There was as much hope of getting them to co-operate as there was of ending the conflict in the Middle East.

Of course, we could make two programmes out of it – Rohauer's Mutual material in one, Rachel Ford's Chaplin material in the other. But what about sequences like the screen test where they were complementary? What about all the new footage from France?

We arranged to meet Rachel to test her reaction. Meanwhile, a *Daily Telegraph* reporter came to interview us about the next batch of *Napoleon* screenings in London. During the lunch, we couldn't resist mentioning the Chaplin project. The following day, a paragraph appeared in the Peterborough column of the *Telegraph*.

Miss Ford, unable to track us down in Perivale, left a message with Shirley that she was "furious". We knew it was probably a good-natured fury, and we recognised how hard it would be to publicise the programmes without mentioning her. But it was tactless of us to mention her name to a reporter, particularly at this critical juncture.

But we had an unexpected ally: *Napoleon*. Rachel Ford had flown over to attend the first screening out of pure friendship. She was expecting to be bored, and hoped to slip out at the first interval – she had taken an aisle seat for this very reason. Instead, the five hours had passed like five minutes, and she had been overwhelmed. Now that we were showing it again, she had persuaded Oona to come and see it, and she returned for a second time. We were further astonished when Mo Rothman ordered seats "for my wife and my ex-wife".

Afterwards, we all gathered at the Rothmans' new home in Pimlico. We felt as if we were entering forbidden territory (the music should have been *In the Hall of the Mountain King*). From the outside, the bandit's lair was unexceptional. The first sign of the unusual was a lift – unusual at least for a four-storey building and the doors opened out to an ad-man's fantasy: glistening mirrors, oriental sculpture, exotic plants, erotic prints and deep-pile carpet. The colours were cool and restful, as was the lighting. Mo was in high good humour, full of praise for the film, for Carl's music and for David's organisation – a role he knew a good deal about. We met his new wife Lynn, tall, young, upper-class English who was equally enthusiastic about what she had just seen. Oona had seen the film in New York, despite our pleas to wait for the London show, when the music would be so much more impressive. "It would have been social death not to have seen it," she laughed. Now she had seen it again, she was understandably surfeited with *Napoleon*, and although she said all the right things, I noticed she seemed in low spirits They seemed to sink further when we began to talk about the Rohauer material. David provided a graphic description of what we had seen: "We never for one moment suspected the rushes would show a complete switch in his thinking," he said, describing *The Cure*. As we tried to impress upon the assembly the importance of the material, our enthusiasm seemed to be making Oona more and more uncomfortable.

I drew David's attention to my suspicions as we left, but he didn't draw the same conclusion. "She is always tired after travelling," he said. "And she's just sat through five hours of *Napoleon*..."

The following evening (3 March 1981) we had dinner with Miss Ford at Rule's Restaurant in Maiden Lane, behind the Strand. Because our wives, Virginia and Pauline, were with us, it was difficult to stick to business, and Miss Ford told us remarkable stories of the war. She did, however, inform us that last night we had left Oona feeling very depressed. She had said, "Charlie wouldn't want this." She was also worried about the fact that on our interview trip to America, we planned to talk to "Lillita" Grey. "She is in low spirits, and has been for some weeks," she explained. It wasn't entirely our project, we gathered but it was clearly causing her a great deal of heart-searching. As for Lita Grey, she explained: "Charlie was not a vindictive man, and he seldom bore a grudge. But not long ago, when we were showing *The Idle Class*, and Lita Grey and her mother came on the screen, he spoke of them in terms of the most extreme dislike. Lita Grey had written a book which had caused a sensation in the mid-sixties.[24] It was one of those 'as told to' books, and it purported to be an account of her marriage to Chaplin. It painted Chaplin in hideous colours, and Lita came out of it like the flirtatious angel she played in *The Kid*. Yet it had the effect on many readers of turning them against Lita Grey; could anyone so vindictive be even vaguely accurate? We intended to interview Lita Grey, for she was an important witness to Chaplin as a filmmaker, and we had no intention of dealing with the marriage. "Mind you," said David, "when we saw the Barry Norman *Hollywood Greats* on Chaplin, I was impressed by Lita Grey."[25] "Well, I warn you," said Miss Ford. "There may be a problem with Oona."

---

24. Lita Grey was unhappy with her 1966 book. Her co-author, a journalist, had encouraged Lita to spice it up and he fabricated things himself. She produced another book, with Jeffrey Vance, which appeared, posthumously, as *Wife of the Life of the Party* (1998).

25. Despite the bitterness, she had ended by saying, "Oona became his stability and she turned out to be a fabulous wife and mother, and I think she brought him a measure of contentment that he'd never had."

13. Over There

We prepared ourselves for the American trip, listing potential interview subjects, a pretty pitiful list compared to what we had on *Hollywood*. We quickly realised that most of the people we needed were dead. Chaplin evidently liked to work with men older than he was – and he would have been 91 had he lived. We were relieved that he liked young women! Jacqui French had joined us as researcher, and it was a very demanding job she had taken on. I had spent thirty years studying silent films, but even so, I would never claim to be an expert on Chaplin. Jacqui had hardly spent as many days. She was young and pretty – which would give her a head start in Hollywood – and she was conscientious and serious. She left for America a week ahead of us.

Both David and I knew we were going too early. The sensible approach would have been to wait for all the Chaplin footage to arrive, and to view it all. Then we would have known exactly what we wanted to ask our interviewees. But I am pessimistic by nature, and I had been suffering from too many surprises from the obituary columns of *Variety*. I remembered, when we started *Hollywood*, that I had drawn up a list of vital people to interview – and eight died within a few weeks. We knew from our research trip that there were three first-class interviews – Virginia Cherrill, Georgia Hale and Dean Riesner. The thought of being prevented from getting any of these three – even by slight illness – haunted me.

We flew over on March 10th 1981 to Los Angeles, and having endured the mundane miseries of air travel – inefficient immigration control leading to endless queues – we booked into our usual hotel, the Continental Hyatt House on Sunset Strip, and checked with Jacqui. Her report was not exactly optimistic. So far, she had found nobody who had worked at Mutual, nobody who had worked with Chaplin as technician at all. It seemed as if everyone who had had anything to do with the Chaplin studios before 1930 had been wiped out – except for a couple who'd been kids at the time ... and our three vital people. Los Angeles had always been a sort of magic city for me. Ever since I had first visited it in 1964, I had had the most uncanny good fortune in finding the people I most wanted to meet. Sometimes it was as simple as looking up the name in the phone book. At other times it took months of detective work. But I never left the place without the feeling that somehow I had been too fortunate. One day, it would be very different. That day had come. First, I rang the all-important Georgia Hale, and was very alarmed when I got through. The voice at the other end sounded like her, and yet she was saying that Georgia wasn't there. "Do you know when she will be?" "Try at six." "She'll be back at six." "Uh-huh." It was that "Uh-huh" and the inflexion with which it was said that convinced me that Georgia Hale was doing a Lillian Gish. During *Hollywood*, Lillian Gish had steadfastly refused to be interviewed; she was doing her own show. Eventually, David urged me to go over to New York and tackle her once and for all. When I called, I heard the one-and-only Lillian Gish answer, but foolishly said, "Is that Miss Gish?" She asked who was calling and said she wasn't in and I should call back at three. At three, of course, her manager was at the other end, ready to field my urgent pleas. What struck me as so funny was that an actress with such a distinctive voice should try to pretend to be someone else. Now that Georgia Hale seemed to be pulling the same stunt I was not in the least amused. At six, of course, there was no answer.

Neither was there any answer from Virginia Cherrill or Dean Riesner. The obvious thing would have been to have called from England to check that everyone was there, and ready to see us. But in my experience, people find it much easier to put you off when you are 6,000 miles away than when you have travelled that distance especially to see them.

This initial failure cast a cloud over a trip Jacqui had arranged to the old Chaplin studios, on La Brea. We had seen this place so often on Miss Ford's material that we felt we knew every inch of it. The shrubbery planted outside the North Circular Road-type cottages had grown so tall the original structure was hardly visible. A historical marker stated that the Chaplin studios dated from 1919 – they are fairly casual about their history in California. It should have been 1917. As a historic monument, the place had to be kept intact, so our guide, a black jazz musician, told us. But there were few signs of conservation. The sound stage had been painted with psychedelic discs whirling across the stucco walls for the current owners, who were A & M Records (Herb Alpert being the A). A new building had been put up and several others altered out of all recognition. The old carpenter's shop had been kept on as a carpenter's shop, producing office furniture, otherwise the visitor would never guess this had been a motion picture studio. The imprint of Chaplin's boots, which he had placed in the wet concrete all those years ago, was fading fast and a flight of steps had been erected perilously close to them.

The swimming pool had been built over, for four recording studios. Yet the place still had that atmosphere of a quiet oasis. Although characters very foreign to the Chaplin days wandered about and stared at us with slightly hostile curiosity – sleek young record producers, and tall black ladies in slacks. Who would have thought, in the days when Chaplin was guest conducting for Abe Lyman's band, that a record company would have taken over a movie studio! It is particularly ironic in the case of Chaplin, who held out against sound for so long.

Whenever we passed a telephone, I tried calling Virginia Cherrill and at last I got through. She was initially hesitant, but she finally agreed that we could go up and see her. She called back to the hotel and suggested we had lunch with her and Eleanor (Eleanor Boardman, the actress), at Montecito. Virginia Cherrill was welcoming. She apologised for a cold sore and a runny nose which, I thought, were going to make the idea of an interview even less attractive. She drove us to pick up Eleanor, who looked very dashing in a flamboyant felt hat, with an original Napoleonic gorget around her neck. Virginia was dressed in a more demure, more English outfit, with a tweed overcoat. We went to the Boat Club for lunch. They were both in a highly gossipy mood, and we were startled to hear some of the more risque stories about early Hollywood. Eleanor had bitter memories of Chaplin, and held that in real life he was the exact opposite of his screen persona. She did not have any stories about his working methods, but recalled one incident: "Chaplin told me that he would feel a scene. He would go to his bathroom, stand in front of a mirror and put two needles in his fingers. He would feel the scene and watch himself, but if he got carried away, he'd stick himself with the needles. He was trying to observe what he was doing so he could do it over and over."

After lunch, we returned to Eleanor's house. In this relaxing environment, David and I confronted Virginia and put it to her bluntly that we wanted to interview her on film. And furthermore, the crew was flying out on Sunday. Virginia was taken aback, but Eleanor supported us: "Do it!" she cried. To our intense relief, Virginia did not put up too much of a fight. When her husband, Florian, heard about it, he said

"Don't go to the hair-dresser. She makes you look like a hen with its wings clipped." We returned to Los Angeles in a much better mood than when we'd driven out. But back at the hotel, Problem No.1: Georgia Hale. I tried calling her again ... no answer. Was she there all the time, and not answering, or was she away? In which case, how long would she be?

Before setting out for California, we had written to the *Los Angeles Times* and *Herald-Examiner* asking for those who had worked with Chaplin to get in touch. They published the letter, together with a photograph.[26] The next day was Friday, March 13th – Friday the Thirteenth with a vengeance. We went over the situation with Jacqui. Very few people had replied to the letter. One woman had worked with Sennett, but Jacqui felt she was of little help. Jacqui had checked the list of "possibles": producer Boris Ingster, who had come over with Eisenstein, and who might have known Chaplin, had died. Child actor Wesley Barry had never worked with Chaplin. Comedienne Billy Rhodes was in poor condition. Cameraman Glen MacWilliams had never worked with Chaplin, and had little to say about Chaplin's relationship with Fairbanks. Clyde Cook, who had known Chaplin in the Karno days, was ill and didn't want to meet anyone. Alice White, star of late silents and early talkies, had worked at the Chaplin studio as script girl, but Jacqui couldn't locate her. Cameraman Karl Struss, who had photographed *The Great Dictator*, was ill and "hardly talks at all". The only hopeful interviewees were Ted Tetrick, who had been Chaplin's assistant on the late pictures, and Eugene Lourié, art director of *Limelight*. From the silent days, there was only a set musician from *The Gold Rush*, Mischa Terr, whose name had been given us by Rohauer.

Here we were, with the crew arriving on Sunday, and all we'd got, as far as the silent era was concerned, was one leading lady from *City Lights*, and a set musician from *The Gold Rush*. It was absurd. Dean Riesner was still unobtainable and Georgia Hale was incommunicado. We decided the best thing we could do was to write Georgia a letter, which David delivered while I tried to drum up some more people via the telephone. I produced little result. But Lisa Mitchell, who was a Chaplin devotee, recalled the name "Dan James" – assistant director. I

---

26. But the *Herald Examiner* forwarded the replies by surface mail. And surface mail took eight weeks!

said I had tried him on the last trip, but drawn a blank. "Well," she said, "I came across a note I'd made that he was last heard of in Carmel." I called Directory Assistance for Carmel and within a few minutes was speaking to Dan James. That's more like it, I thought. That was the response I was accustomed to in Hollywood!

"I can't tell you how delighted I am to have found you," I said, full of optimism But this wasn't Friday the Thirteenth for nothing. I explained what we were doing, and he said, "Oh no, I wouldn't appear on the tube, old boy. I have an aversion to seeing myself and I wouldn't like to inflict this face on the rest of the world. I'd be happy to do a tape... but you'd have to drive up here." "I completely sympathise with your attitude," I said, through gritted teeth "But you can understand my position." "Yes," he said, simply. . .You must be hating me." He said he had been in on the scripting of *The Great Dictator*, he became the assistant director and he went right through the editing stage. He recalled scenes that weren't used. "We did some wonderful experiments with a one-man blimp – with Charlie's arms and legs sticking out. That was the funniest thing I've ever seen." He added, "I was the sole secretary and I helped with the script. I went right through the production and I was kept on all through the cutting. I can tell you all about his method of approaching a scene, and the curious jealousy between him and Jack Oakie. I can describe his political thinking at the time. I have a copy of the script – it is twice as long as the final picture. I went through the entire two-year experience. My memories are very pleasant, although not as sharp as they used to be." No, he wouldn't travel from Carmel; he said the trip by car was six and a half hours. Nor would he fly down; he was working on a novel. So we left it like that *The Great Dictator* was outside the scope of the programme – although we expected the next consignment to include out-takes from it. We planned to concentrate on Chaplin as a silent filmmaker.

Dan James would just have to wait.[27]

David returned from delivering the letter to Georgia Hale to report that the house was barricaded with bars on doors and windows, but – and this was an important but – there was a padlock catch on the door which anyone going away for any length of time would secure. It was

27. Fortunately, David Robinson interviewed him for his Chaplin biography and we used the tape in *The Tramp and the Dictator* (2002).

open. This depressed me even more than I was already, because it convinced me that Georgia was doing a Lillian Gish. I had written to her before we left, indicating when we hoped to arrive, and mentioning how much we looked forward to seeing her again, and to reading her manuscript.

David had some more news. He had spoken to our Head of Documentaries in London, Mike Wooller, about the BAFTA awards. *Hollywood* had been nominated in the documentary category. No, he said, we hadn't won. What he failed to tell me that afternoon would enliven things a few days hence. Coming back on the freeway that night, David suggested taking a later exit and cruising down La Brea to Georgia's home. "You never know," he said. "There may be a light on." There was. He pulled in to the nearest telephone and I found myself speaking to a young man. "Is Georgia in?" I asked. "Er – I don't know," he said, hesitantly. "That's strange," I said. "Is she out?" "Er – I don't know." "Do you know when she might be coming back?" "Er – I don't know."

By this time, I was convinced she was sitting there, shaking her head and putting her finger to her lips and the fellow wasn't able to make much sense. Either that, or I'd disturbed a burglar.

Another problem was Dean Riesner. He was still not answering his phone. A day or two wasn't worrying, but after four days we began to suspect he had gone on location with his latest picture. That could mean weeks before he returned. We sent him a telegram – still no answer. I was now convinced that coming early was not merely inadvisable, but was a major error. David managed to persuade the crew to stay an extra day on their Atlanta assignment; we had to round up more people.

We visited Lita Grey Chaplin. She was pleasant and reasonable, but she was also anxious about how our project might conflict with a projected film of her book.

We returned to the hotel, and there was a message from Dean Riesner. His phone had been out of order and he'd been in all the time. He said he'd be delighted to do the interview whenever we were ready; he sounded genuinely enthusiastic.

Another of David's schemes now paid off. Jacqui had taken flowers round to Georgia's house at his suggestion, with a note saying, "What did we do wrong? Your two unhappy English admirers." Jacqui reported that a dark-skinned, middle-aged man had come to the door. He had said he would see if she was in, but he had reappeared without her.

Shortly afterwards, this man telephoned me. He said his name was Mr Herman, that he was "the manager" and it was impossible to see Miss Hale.

"She is looking after her sister, who is ill. But she said you could pick up her manuscript."

Well, that was a tiny chink of light. We drove round immediately, and Mr Herman greeted us. The parcel was right behind him on the porch, so there was no question of his inviting us in.

"There's a letter in there," he said. We emphasised how anxious we were to see Georgia. "How long do you think she'll be away?" asked David. "Who knows? Three days... three weeks."

We did all we could to assure him that the only thing we wanted in life was to see Georgia (and at that moment, that was true!) and off we went, clutching our parcel. In the car, we opened the parcel and read the letter. It had been written that very day, so she must have been there at some point. "Thank you for the beautiful flowers. So thoughtful of you. I am being nurse, doctor, housemaid – everything – to a younger sister. So I'm completely busy without a moment to myself until this passes. Kevin, here is my manuscript. I always wanted to submit it to Woody Allen – to me he is the perfect one to do Charlie. If you want to read it and if you think it has any merit – I'd be happy to let you do what you think best. Any way you think it should be handled it would be all right. What do you think could be worked out for me?" I remembered how much she admired Ivor Montagu, and I had ended the last note with the remark that he was working closely with us. "I just love Hell and Ivor and I'm happy they are working closely with you – we all have one thing in common – we love Charlie. With great expectations, Georgia Hale."

The manuscript was a fascinating record of her experiences with Chaplin; it contained so much remarkable information that it made an interview with her even more crucial. It showed what Chaplin's films had meant to a girl born into poverty, suffering from hopelessness and despair. She had fallen in love with him from his first appearance on the screen. His optimism gave her optimism, and the fact that she became his leading lady gave her memoirs the quality of a fairy story.[28] She later

---

28. They have since been published by Scarecrow Press.

became a Christian Scientist. Her strictures on dealing with hopeless situations gave me hope. I could not believe she would let us down.

David suggested a trip to Palm Springs to check out Jackie Coogan and Sydney Chaplin. Coogan was as affable as ever, and told us he intended doing a remake of *The Kid* with himself in the Chaplin role and his grandson in his part. Sydney, on the other hand, was maddeningly elusive. When we eventually met him, he said he did all he could to avoid work so he could spend his time on the golf course.

While in Palm Springs, a Chaplinesque experience occurred in a restaurant. I lost my hotel key. I dropped by the restaurant to ask if they had found it. A waitress told me to enquire at the back, and with immaculate timing, her gesturing hand struck the tray of a passing waiter. Two glasses of chilled white wine flooded down the back of a dowager seated nearby, and as she rose, she yelled.

"Are you hurt, madame?" asked the waiter.

"No!" she shrieked. "I'm WET!!!" We felt Charlie had his eye on us.

Back in Los Angeles, David rang Sydney's agent and was staggered to learn that he expected $10,000 for an interview. He had to waste crucial hours in phone call after phone call before he had reduced the demand to a still outrageous $5,000. (The average for interviews was $400.) And Sydney wasn't the only one. Martha Raye's agent wanted $3,000 merely to talk to her about *Monsieur Verdoux*. To film her would be another deal.

14. Celtic Twilight

March 17th was our lowest point. It was St Patrick's Day and the fellow giving us the most trouble was the Irishman, Tim Durant. David had already had a lot of trouble with him over the fee. He turned his nose up at $500, which we knew was $100 more than the BBC had paid him. ("Yes, but the BBC was only for the UK," he had said, cannily.) He demanded $1,500. What was the matter with all these people? Was it the name Chaplin that turned their minds into cash registers?

"I've given you so much of my time already," Durant said to David. "What you're doing will conflict with my book. I gave you that long interview. I know I shouldn't have done it. You're going to take everything from me, I know. What are you going to do with that tape? Are you going to give it to me?"

"We aren't going to use it."

"Why did you do it, then? I don't like the way this whole thing is being done. You can manage without me. I'm going to pull out. You don't need me at all."

David suggested I took over, in an attempt to calm him down and try to show that his fears were groundless. I did not do very well.

"I hear you're not very happy with us."

"No, I'm not. And I'm backing out. I've got a lot of problems. I'm not in good shape. I'm 81 years old and I just don't need all this. You're manipulating me and using me..."

"We're making a tribute to a friend of yours."

"That's bullshit. You're a commercial operation." It was the money that had upset him. Presumably he saw his value reflected in our fee, and thus the value of the book that he couldn't bring himself to write. He returned to the subject of the tape – what were we going to do with it... why didn't we give it back?

"Would that set your mind at rest?" I asked.

"Not talking to you would set my mind at rest," he snarled. When his paranoia had reached excess, I interrupted him. "Mr Durant!" I said, "you are a practising Christian!"

"Yes I am," he said, "but that doesn't apply in this case."

We considered asking Oona to intercede on our behalf; we even called Switzerland only to discover she wasn't there. Eventually, David wrote a letter to Durant to calm his fears. And to cut him out of the programme. On top of all this, I rang Virginia in London. "Are you coming back?" she said. I explained that since *Hollywood* had not won the BAFTA award, we would not be whisked over by Thames for the ceremony. She choked back something, and I sensed a plot. Eventually, and under duress, she told me that I was being given the Michael Balcon award. This had quite the opposite effect than the organisers intended. It maddened me. *Hollywood* was as much David's project as it was mine; in some aspects, more so. I hated being singled out. I hated even more the idea of returning to London in the middle of this struggle for interviews. A ten-hour flight to England, and a return flight of twelve hours to California, with all the jet lag which that entailed, was hardly what I needed. When Mike Wooller called from London to ask me to return I refused point blank.

Since the crew had arrived, and we were still facing an extremely meagre list of interviewees, I decided to spend the whole of Tuesday, which happened to be their rest day, on the telephone. A film historian friend, George Mitchell, had recommended an old cameraman called Hans Koenekamp, who had worked at Sennett. Jacqui, and another historian friend, Marc Wanamaker, drove off to see him. I regretted not being able to go with them, for I had never met him, and Koenekamp's work featured in *Hollywood*. I spent the whole day imprisoned in the half light of the gloomy hotel room, furiously trying to drum up some trade on the telephone. In vain.

We drove in convoy to Montecito, to interview Virginia Cherrill. The suspense was tangible as we approached her secluded house; what excuse would she have for turning us away? A sign on the door said PLEASE COME IN, so we did. As we entered her cool, spacious living room, which looked on to the calm oasis of a garden, she made a stunning entrance. She looked extremely attractive in a simple blue dress, and her manner was so warm that we relaxed at once. She did admit that she had dreaded the whole thing and was going to call us to put it off. "But I lacked the guts," she added. The interview was excellent; it ran over the same points she had made on our previous visit, but she was more positive about Chaplin. Afterwards, she served us tea and sandwiches, and showed us pictures of her years in England, taken by *Life* photographers, or Beaton. There was even a group by Steichen. David and I each selected a duplicate and asked her to sign them. The next thing we noticed was that every member of the crew had the same large, original and often valuable studio portraits. She was handing them out to whoever asked for them, and I was charmed to see assistant cameraman Paul Cavanagh sitting on a settee staring at his picture, absolutely enchanted by it.

Virginia Cherrill refused a fee. After a great deal of persuasion, she accepted it, then rang me next morning to say she and Florian had discussed it and decided they couldn't take it and would we please use it to give the crew an outing?

March 19th. A short trip out to David Raksin in the Valley. Raksin had worked with Chaplin on the music for *Modern Times*. We walked up to his house and through the mesh of the screen door found ourselves staring at Raksin at work. When he heard the knock, he jumped up. "As Clifton Webb says in *Laura*, 'It's lavish, but it's home.'" His house was a bungalow, open plan, his working area dominated by a large piano and piles of papers and magazines and scripts and letters in what resembled order, but what one suspected was hopeless confusion. He showed us a caricature of him by Chaplin (and there was a doodle by Gershwin beneath). The walls were lined with the usual cluster of awards, in brick pigeon holes.

David ran over the areas arising out of an article Gershwin had loaned us, and he was responsive. But he came alive once the camera was on him, and rather ran away with the first magazine – one question led to a seven-minute answer! There was a marvellous moment when he described Chaplin coming in one morning with a phrase of music – he played it and one could recognise what it was. Then he demonstrated how they developed it into the theme that became known as *Smile*. Trouble was, the magic dissipated when we realised he couldn't play the piano very well. Raksin seemed surprised to be offered a fee. At first he refused it, then I suggested he used it for his piano (which he had complained was going to cost a fortune to be overhauled). Then he thanked us and said, "I'll use it to revive Tallulah Bankhead and keep her."

David Raksin

As far as I was concerned, Chaplin was the most important person in movies, as a director, writer, and actor, and I loved everything he did. My dad was a conductor for silent pictures for quite a while and I used to go every Saturday and sit beside him in the pit and watch what he did with his orchestra in accompanying silent films. I would say all the time, "Some day I'm going to write for movies."

In that celebrated projection room of his at his studio on La Brea, I was introduced to Charlie. He was very charming and very friendly. When Charlie decided he wanted to charm somebody, you had better look out. So in no time at all, I was not only a devoted fan, but I was absolutely overwhelmed by being in the man's presence. Well, he showed me the movie and he sat next to me, and after a while I got embarrassed, because I was laughing so much during the feeding machine sequence that I thought he might believe that I was exaggerating. I just couldn't help myself – my stomach was actually hurting from laughing, because I'd never seen anything like it. He must have been gratified that I was affected in that way by his movie, and so we started off on a very good footing.

Charlie would come in at about ten o'clock. I'd be in my own office, which was a little room near the projection room in which we both worked. Carter De Haven Jr., who is now a producer, and was the son of one of Charlie's intimates, would come running in and say "He's here!" and when he did that everybody was supposed to drop whatever they were doing and run. Well, I was rather ornery about that, so I made sure that I let a decent interval intervene between the time I was told to appear and the time I actually appeared. I'd walk in. He'd be striding up and down. His head would be full of music which he'd been thinking about, and he'd have little musical ideas which he would then play for me – he'd play with one finger on the piano – and I'd take the idea and write it down. Sometimes I'd talk to him about whether or not I considered that the idea was appropriate for that place in the film, which, as I've often thought, is absolutely appalling chutzpah. You know, the sheer nerve of some squirt of 21 or 22 having the gall to tell this great man what was appropriate for his own film was ridiculous. But I wanted to make sure that the music for that film was just about as good as it could possibly have been. As far as I was concerned, the best composer in the world would not have been too good for Charlie and the film. So I argued with him a bit and the result of these arguments was that after about a week and a half he finally fired me. He wasn't used to have anybody disagree with him. He always had his own way and everybody would bend to his will. So he fired me. It was a terrible blow, I just fell apart. [Through the good offices of Alfred Newman, Raksin was called back to the studio to be re-hired.] I said I couldn't do it unless I had an understanding with Charlie, otherwise the same thing will only happen right away again. So it was arranged that I would have a session with

Charlie, which went on for several hours. I didn't want anyone there, so that anything I said to Charlie in frankness could be construed as being fresh or sarcastic. I explained to him that I thought he already had his share of people who were all too eager to "yes" him and that if he needed a musical secretary he could find one anywhere, he didn't need me. But if he wanted somebody who cared enough about him and his picture to fight him tooth and nail where it was necessary without any thought of personal ego, but just really because he cared, then I would love to work with him. And he put his arms around me and hugged me and we started off and we worked for four and a half months that way, arguing, fighting – I'd stalk out of the room sometimes and he'd send Carter after me. "I can't go back," I'd say, "I'm going to punch him on the nose." But somehow we got along. It became a sort of father and son thing. He was trying to educate me away from my innocence. I loved the picture, and I loved working with him. I found him the most entertaining person I've ever met in my life.

Charlie was not a musician, but he had musical ideas galore, and once the idea was written down he also had a very large share in determining where it would go. He even had ideas concerning the orchestration. I remember we got into a kind of a funny conversation about who should play a certain melody. I think it was just a thing that went like this [Raksin demonstrates on piano]. And I said, well, I don't know exactly what you're thinking, Charlie, originally we talked about doing this on a bassoon. He said, no, it sounds too sissified. So I said, well it doesn't sound right on the trombone, it sounds too heavy and I don't think the

French horn should play this and it certainly is not for strings according to what you're doing on the screen. We finally agreed a tenor saxophone to play it and that's what plays it in the picture. But the very fact that he was able to do that and visualise the sound, I mean to hear it in his ear, is marvellous and something few people understand – when you're orchestrating, you're hearing what the instrument sounds like.

When he came to one place in the film which had to do with Paulette, he said what we need here is a sort of a Puccini tune, which did not mean that he was going to use one of Puccini's tunes, or actually steal one, but that he wanted a tune in that style. And he went home and the next morning he came with the following tune which went like this. [He played a version of *Smile*.] And so we took that and played around with it and developed it and it eventually turned out to be something like this. [He played *Smile* as we know it.] Eventually, as you know, that became a popular song. Charlie was a guy with a mind like an attic, and in this mind all kinds of things accumulated, dating from his early days. There were various things which came from his musical comedy days, and that was the predominant musical structure in his mind.

He played the piano some, he played the violin, he played the cello – there's a picture of him playing the cello on the cover of some piece he wrote called *Oh, That Cello!* And he also played the organ. When I went up to his house he played the organ for me a little. Had I not been a musician, he might have been less intimidated, but he did play a little just to let me know that he had a real no-kidding organ in his house and it was sort of fun.

> Henry Bergman told me about a time Charlie was at a party and he suddenly launched into this Russian basso aria and he sang it with all his vim and vigour and somebody said, "I didn't know you could sing," and he said, "I can't. I was imitating Chaliapin."

The Georgia Hale problem was still uppermost in our minds, and now that I had been persuaded to return to London, we decided to use that fact as ammunition in our campaign. At David's suggestion, I wrote a letter at David Raksin's saying that I was having to return to London tomorrow – could I see her before I left, if only to return the manuscript? David drove me round while the crew were at lunch, and we optimistically rang her bell. No one answered, so I left the letter together with my number at the hotel.

That afternoon, in a tropical downpour, we filmed Dean Riesner, who repeated his splendid story about *The Pilgrim*, and who showed us a scrap-book made for him in 1934 by his father, who had written some touching notes in it: "Dink – I hope this give you the same kick later that it's giving me now."

We drove back as the downpour reached its height and the storm drains couldn't cope. Vehicles sent water in vicious arcs across the road. Pedestrians had to take their shoes off and wade through the gutters to reach the sidewalk, only to be drenched by the cars. Back at the hotel, no messages. Nothing from Georgia. No reply from her number.

March 20th: Durant had been pencilled in today, so we tried to substitute cameraman Hans Koenekamp, but he backed out, too, pleading sickness. On top of which King Vidor had to back out because of a court case. So today we went to see Eugene Lourié, who had been art director on *Limelight*. A diminutive figure, slightly hunched, yet with an expansive confidence and a sense of humour that belied his meek appearance, Lourié was a Russian who had worked in France, and had been art director on several Jean Renoir films, including *La Grande Illusion*. He had first encountered Chaplin when he lived in Turkey.

Eugene Lourié

I first saw the Chaplin films in Istanbul, in a small theatre where I worked as a kind of publicity man. I used to live in a little room above the audience. Each time, when the piano player played a gay tune, I knew it was a comedy and a Chaplin comedy was announced by a tremendous roar from the audience. I'd run down to look again and again at the picture. Now the Turkish audience is much more temperamental than the European or American, and it was really almost like a riot. Many years later, I was coming back from India, from the picture *The River* with Renoir and a production manager called me. He says "Do you know London?" I said, yes, I worked on a Russian play in the Alhambra Theatre, Leicester Square in 1933. "Okay. I will pick you up tomorrow morning and we will go to the producer."

He never mentioned the name of the producer. When we were in the car driving to Beverly Hills, he said, "We will see Charlie Chaplin." Ah, I said, goodness! It was a thrill. I admired Chaplin very much but I had never met him. So we went to this quiet street and a butler in white took us through the house to the back terrace and there was Charlie Chaplin eating his breakfast. I was admiring the very elegant and precise movements where he's cutting the cutlets. It reminded me of the scene in *The Gold*

Rush when, with the same elegance and precision, he was cutting the shoe.

He explained roughly about the picture, saying that the picture will be shot in Hollywood but the locale is London and he's very keen to have a kind of authentic atmosphere, not authentic in architectural terms, but authentic in the feeling of this middle-class London.

He started to work with a German art director who was very good, but seemingly the first sketches he showed were kind of heavy, they didn't have the spirit of London, so he asked me. He said would I agree to work for two weeks, kind of reading over the script, getting together my ideas, and speaking with him again two weeks later? And then we would decide if we would do the picture together. Well, I found this very reasonable because it's very strange, really, especially in Hollywood, very often you are put together with a director that you've never met, and finally you are married together, and so I thought it was very good to have a kind of trial period.

[Lourié also remembered a visit to the studio by the Royal Ballet – among whom was a young dancer called David Gill.] Next time I met Chaplin we spoke about it, and he asked me what I remembered from London, and I told him how amazed I was, first seeing it in 1933, at the sadness of the Victorian uniformity in the streets in lower class London, and he said, "That's exactly that. If you like, Mr Lourié, we'll start to work together." To build a street in his own studio was very expensive, for relatively short scenes, so we looked for existing streets. I looked in many studios and finally I thought Paramount's New York street was the best one. It was a kind of nondescript street of uniform buildings with stairways outside. He accepted it and we made the street there, for Calvero's house, and the street also where he runs for the doctor when he finds Claire Bloom in his room, and the scenes with the pub where his friends played in the small orchestra, and later on where he played himself in front of the pub. For him the most important was the floorplan of the set. For me also, it was the most important. I never start a picture by drawing a sketch, I always started with the floorplan, because the floorplan is where the actor will move, and where the camera will move. For him the floorplan was important because he directed his actors almost like dancers. The first set I built for him almost immediately because he wanted to rehearse with Claire Bloom for at least four weeks. The second day he said, "Mr Lourié, is it possible to enlarge the room? I need about 18 inches more between the door and the stove. I need one more step." All my walls had an extra two or three feet and I told him it could be ready tomorrow because I only had to move the walls. Since that day, our relations were much better. In the pantomime scene, I had only one set, a painted backing built-in flat with the ceiling, with very strong false perspective. When we started to shoot the picture, he says, "Let's rehearse the moving of the set," I said, "Why?" "We will rehearse because I need to do it in exactly 18 seconds." I say, "Mr Chaplin, I don't know, maybe it will take 18, maybe 20 or 17." "No, I wrote the music already and the music is exactly 18 seconds, so let's try and shoot it. If we guessed right and it is 18 seconds, we can use it. If not, put back the set."

We shot it. The first day it was good and that was that.

> As you know, in silent days they very often shot scenes with background music playing. It was done for the mood of the picture, and probably also it gives a certain rhythm, a certain tempo for acting. Chaplin was accustomed from silent days to have music while he is acting. In fact it was the only way to do the scenes like his songs, because his songs were like little dances and you cannot dance without music.

After the Lourié interview, I left for England, staying just for the weekend. When I returned, I discovered that David had spoken to Mr Herman, explaining that, while I was away, there might be some anxiety over the manuscript. Herman was unimpressed. "I know it's in safe hands," he said, flatly. David put in a plug for the Divinity and linked him with our project: "We must put our trust in God and in each other!" Herman was equally unimpressed when I called him. "Is Georgia back?"

"No," I explained, "it's impossible to see her. She'll answer any questions but it's impossible to talk to her."

"Well, I'm back at the same hotel, and I'm very anxious indeed to hear from her." He took careful note of the number.

Then down we went to Palm Springs, in temperatures of ninety plus, to interview Jackie Coogan. He came up with none of the emotional moments this time – how could he when he'd hit such a bullseye in *Hollywood*? But he presented his recollections in an intelligent and interesting way. Sydney Chaplin, in between rounds of golf, gave us an excellent interview, which suggested that his acting talent had never been properly exploited. But then his image was that of a debonair, handsome individual who couldn't be bothered to work. And what better gift could such a driven man as Chaplin have left to at least one son than guiltless indolence?

Sydney Chaplin

He never talked much about his work, it's funny, to anybody. I don't know if you ever noticed that. He said once that comedy is just getting people into and out of trouble. He worked at the house in the afternoon and if he got excited, well, he'd bore everyone in the family, because he'd grab you and test out the idea on you. He usually knew it was good without asking but he liked it to be reaffirmed that it was a good scene or a funny idea. He used to get angry if he went on vacation. He'd say "I'm wasting my time. I should be working." Oona would have to jam him into the car and say "Look, Charlie, two weeks doesn't hurt you." He was grumbling and yelling.

I remember how *Limelight* started. It started as a completely different story. He had an idea about a man very jealous of his wife. A clown is peeking through the hole in the curtain and he sees his wife flirting with a man in the audience. That wasn't at all in the story, but he started from that and then he stimulated it himself and then the story got to a certain point and he said, "Well, that stinks."

He had an enormous self-discipline. And the days nothing happened he was enormously depressed, and the days it was good, I think that was his biggest joy in life, more than actually the picture coming out and the success and everything else. I remember when *City Lights* opened and it was a smash hit – lines around the corner, rave reviews – he had a deep depression and he said, "What am I going to do next?" Which was a thousand per cent him. That's just the way he was. So it was a man who was never really content with whatever he did. Most people have a success and they live off it for ten years, you know.

Limelight was the first picture I ever did in my life. Working with him, you were charged all the time. I've worked on pictures where I couldn't keep my eyes open, but you're always stimulated when he was excited. You couldn't be sitting around, that was impossible. Sometimes on a long day some of the grips, who weren't involved and didn't know the story that well, would get tired and it used to make him furious – he'd be doing a funny routine and he'd see a guy watching, with a bored expression, chewing gum. He'd say, "Quick, get that man's face out of here." He was very sensitive to reaction.

At the end of a scene, he'd first look at the cameraman, and say, "Is it all right? Nothing went wrong?" If he thought he did it well and there was a technical fault, he went crazy. A script girl was murder for him because he would do something very, very funny and she'd suddenly notice that the window was open in one scene and in the next it was closed. That he didn't care about, strangely enough, he would never get sore, where a lot of directors would have said, "God, the thing was on the table, now it's not on the table." He said "If they're looking at that we've got a stinking scene and if it's really funny they shouldn't care." And it's true. If you look carefully at his pictures and you're looking just for faults, you'll see nine million things.

The English language hampered him and he always said silent pictures are the true art form of movies. The true beauty of the picture is what people imagine. Try to put words at the end of *City Lights*. I mean, anything they said would have been terrible. Whereas you were left torn – did she go with him? Did she care about him? Did they see each other again? There was an old guy on *Limelight* who was a real old timer, and he had one line. It was the scene after Calvero lays an egg and he comes back into the dressing room and everyone's uncomfortable and one guy says, "These shoes don't fit." This guy was terrified, you could see how frightened he was, and my father saw that, so he could easily have said, "We'll get somebody else." They shot it once and the man was very stiff and uncomfortable. He said "Wonderful, print it." Meanwhile, he told the cameraman, "Don't change anything, we're going to do it again." And he went over and sat in his chair and the man came over.

"Oh, Mr Chaplin," he said. "I was so nervous. I wanted to do a little bit more of something like this... " And he said, "Listen, just for fun, let's do it the way you want to do it. Maybe it's better than what I had." By this time, the man was so relaxed he did it absolutely normally. A simple little scene, but he knew that the man was impossible if he didn't make him relax and feel good.

We drove back to Los Angeles, stopping en route at a restaurant where we discussed our strategy for Georgia Hale. I tried ringing again, and found myself talking to Mr Herman.

"How is Georgia's sister?"

"Much better."

"Oh good. Is there any chance we could see her? Our time is

running out."

"When are you leaving?"

"Sunday," I lied.

"Well, perhaps Saturday."

"Marvellous. I'll call you to check."

"Yes. Call me Friday night."

The news revived David, who was slumped, head in hands, over his coffee. Next morning, at breakfast, Jacqui showed us that her announcement had appeared in the Calendar section of the *LA Times*: CHAPLIN DATA WANTED. And it led to a spate of phone calls – Bob Clampett, the famous animator, recalled being on the set of *The Circus*, but couldn't remember anything specific. Someone remembered Chaplin from his days at Niles, with Essanay. An actress called Ida May had a test of herself with Chaplin. Jacqui went off to pursue these leads, while we went out to interview Norman Lloyd, another actor from *Limelight*. Lloyd was the Alistair Cooke type, with the studied accents of stage elocution. He had been born in New York, but had started his career with Eve Le Gallienne, who had insisted on her players speaking "proper stage English" so they could tackle anything, including classical roles. His impressive house at Brentwood was full of photographs, including a rare one of Oona Chaplin doubling Claire Bloom in *Limelight*.

Norman Lloyd

Chaplin sensed that it was getting increasingly difficult to make people laugh. Now, he always realised that that was difficult. I remember his telling me that when he was doing *City Lights*, which is in some ways reputed to be the funniest that he's ever done, as well as the most moving, he would often sit in his dressing room all day long waiting for an idea to come that would be funny.

Charlie understood that you're as great an artist as you can face the truth that you understand, or the truth that you see. It's not given to all of us. We may be able to see it, but not be able to deal with it as artists and he understood that. In *Limelight*, which is about a comic who can no longer make people laugh, he told that story. And he would say, "I, Charlie Chaplin, doubt that I can make people laugh any longer."

Charlie believed that what separated the men from the boys in our profession was the personal story that the individual had to tell. In the entire look of his pictures, by the rooms that he would dress, the sets that he would have the art director execute, he knew exactly what he wanted. They would all end up with this particular look, which was a special world. And it was the world of a newcomer to this country, poor and struggling to find a place here, and that's the way it always seemed to me. The pictures had a kind of European look, a kind of tenement look so that they would be recognisable, perhaps, in a big city like New York. It didn't look like anybody else's world; there was no other director who ever had a picture look like Charlie's pictures.

One night we went down to the studio and we went into the cottage that had his dressing room and I just couldn't resist it. I opened the closet, and I saw one of the canes. And I thought, "Well, Norman, this is the time you're going to steal this cane." I reached in and began to lift it out. I hadn't figured a way of getting it out of there when Charlie came up beside me and said, "Ah yes," and gently took it from me and just put it back. I had the feeling I wasn't the first one who had tried that. As he put it back, I looked down and came upon one of his secrets. There were the oversized shoes, the most famous shoes in the world. But in the oversized shoes was another pair of shoes, which were the correct size for Charlie's feet, so that when he walked the most famous walk in the world, in the oversized shoes, he actually was in another pair of shoes which gave him the control.[29]

He always felt that he had to work every day. This is virtually a quote of his – if he did not work every day, he did not deserve his dinner. By work, that meant not that he was acting, but writing a script or working on music, which he would go to when the writing work would find a block.

I once saw him quite angrily say to his son Michael, who was five or six – he was dragging a sweater on the floor. He said, "Pick that up off the floor. That was earned."

I heard that Charlie kept about thirty people on salary over the years – people from the silent days. That would include Edna Purviance, Henry Bergman, the gatekeeper at the studio and Rollie Totheroh, his cameraman, and others. He was a generous man, a kind man, although he was not a man who would permit himself to be taken advantage of.

I think that Charlie was in enormous creative conflict at the point that I knew him. With age coming on, would his image dim? It was a very beautiful image, as *Verdoux* is so handsome and beautiful, but it wasn't the image of the tramp which people kept wanting him to do and about which he said, "I have said everything

---

29. Ted Tetrick, who owned a pair of these shoes, told us they were worn on the wrong feet. There was a hole in the heel which he thought was to enable the shoes to be bolted to the floor for trick work. (We prefer to believe the hole was a relic of the roller-skating scene in *The Rink*.) These shoes, along with a hat and cane, were auctioned in London in 1987.

I can with the tramp." He never wanted to do it again, although people like James Agee wrote treatments for him to do the tramp. Now as time went on, his story changed, and the doubt grew larger. And he was working in great chunks of dialogue. This was not his natural medium. He got very angry when he showed *Verdoux* to Clifford Odets and he said "Charlie, it's marvellous, but the dialogue isn't what it should be." And out went Odets. But that was only momentary. They were very good friends, and it was easily patched up.

This was the strongest ego I've ever encountered, put at the service of an art. This ego ordained that everything Charlie did was interesting, even if he threw it out. Everything was interesting simply because he did it, and it so happened that in this case, that was right.

I know it seems like hero-worship on my part, but even if it was unusable, there was something fascinating about everything he did, and it would turn up somewhere else in another form.

15. Too Good to Last

Jacqui told us that a call resulting from the newspaper article had led to one "Mary O'Brien", which meant nothing to any of us. "You must go and see her," said the informant, "because she knows everything. She was Chaplin's secretary." But Chaplin's secretary was Nellie Bly Baker, not Mary O'Brien. And so we were less than enthusiastic about a trip to Bishop, California, four hundred miles away, on the Nevada border. Her phone was permanently busy, so we could not talk to her first. Furthermore, Jacqui had booked her flight back to London. However, she came down to breakfast one morning and informed us that Mrs O'Brien *was* Nellie Bly Baker. Not only had she been Chaplin's secretary, she was in *The Kid* and she played the unforgettable masseuse in *A Woman of Paris*.

David told Jacqui to cancel her flight to London and to take a plane to Bishop. Meanwhile, we carried on with our interviews. David Bradley enabled us to meet Lita Grey.

On the board in the entrance hall of her apartment building was the name "Lita Grey Chaplin". She was an impressive woman. Well into her seventies, she was still working (at Robinson's department store). She struck us as intelligent and honest – none of us could explain that book of hers, unless it was a show business stunt engineered by others.

During the interview, the camera broke down repeatedly, but Lita Grey was not troubled in the least. During one of these maddening breaks, she let me into the secret of her youthful appearance; a face lift at 58. "The best time to do it. It's the time most women are most worried by their appearance. It may last five years. After that you just let it go!"

Lita Grey

I think I was about six years old. My grandmother used to take me down to the Westlake district on a Saturday afternoon to see *The Perils of Pauline* and Charlie Chaplin. Oh, he was such an idol, especially with the children. And it wasn't too long after that that I was taken by the hand in a restaurant to meet the great Charlie Chaplin. He was seated at a table, having lunch with a friend, in the tramp outfit, and it frightened me a little bit, because I couldn't kind of put the two people together – the man I saw on the screen with this man who was real. So it kind of scared me and I ran back to the table, to my mother.

A family by the name of Riesner lived down the block from us when I was about twelve, here in Hollywood, and they had a baby they called Dinky who was eighteen months old, and I used to go to the house and play with the baby. And one day, Chuck Riesner was walking down the same street with Charlie and he called me over and said, "Charlie, this is the little girl I've been telling you about." Charlie said to me, "Would you like to be in a movie?" And I said, "Oh, I'd love to, but I have to find if it's all right with my mother."

She came down and talked to them and it was all arranged and in a few days we were signed in the Chaplin studio on a contract. I became his flirting sweetheart in the heaven sequence of *The Kid*. Charlie had been experimenting with me, putting my hair up on the top of my head, and he had the wardrobe lady dress me in my mother's clothes and I was photographed quite a bit older. I came round the corner, sticking a very skinny leg out, in a flirtatious kind of way. He did a lot of retakes on that because they had trouble on the pulleys – the wiring that pulled everybody up and down. Not only he but some other people flew off a brick wall – I guess it must have been about fourteen feet high – and the men holding the wires slipped

– he fell right on his stomach. He just got the wind knocked out of him a little bit.

He was very nice to us. Jackie Coogan and I liked to swim in the pool, and Charlie swam with us, he laughed and had fun with us and treated us like most people treat children.

The Idle Class was made in the middle of *The Kid*. He suspended work on *The Kid*. I think he lost his inspiration at some point, so he said, "Well, we'll just pick this up later." My mother and I played French maids in it, with old-fashioned bonnets tied under the chin.

My girlfriend was Merna Kennedy, she did the lead in *The Circus*. She'd been a dancer and had been in vaudeville with her brother. Anyway, I was bragging to Merna when I went back to school after I finished *The Kid* contract. I was bragging about having worked for Charlie and what a marvellous man he was, and she wanted to meet him, so I said, "We'll go over to the studio and watch him work one day," which we did. As soon as Charlie came out to greet us, he said, "You're just in time, because I've been testing brunettes for a part in this film I'm going to make." (*The Gold Rush*) So he did another film test on me and decided that I would be right for the part. A funny thing happened before we got up to Truckee (the location). Sid Grauman came down to the train to say goodbye and Charlie held him on the train. He didn't have a toothbrush or a change of clothes and he went all the way to Truckee with us and he stayed the whole trip – I think we were up there two or three weeks.

Charlie was extremely dedicated and the scene in *The Gold Rush* where he eats the shoe – that was liquorice, that shoe, and he and Mack Swain got violently ill from eating so many of these shoes, day after day. I remember him coming home and how sick he was and they called off production for several days.

Charlie had an objective view towards his work. When he commented on it, you didn't feel it was out of vanity, but out of an objective view of whether it was funny or not. He was really very involved in the projection room when he would see the rushes. He would laugh at some things that he was doing himself. He was his own best audience. At other times, "Oh no, we'll have to do that again. Oh, that's very bad. I can't use that." Of course there were many sides to Chaplin. He was moody, temperamental and impatient, when he wasn't working. When he was working he was just a very light-hearted and very happy soul, particularly when he was in makeup in the tramp outfit. I'll never forget the first time I saw him as a civilian, without makeup, one day at his house, and the next day at the studio when he came out of the dressing room as the tramp. It was just unbelievable. Charlie was an entirely different person. So he lived really in two worlds.

I couldn't have finished *The Gold Rush* because I was pregnant and they couldn't have photographed me at a later time. So he looked for someone that had my general colouring, dark hair, and dark eyes and Georgia Hale and I looked very much alike. As a matter of fact, the book that I wrote that went to press in 1965 had a picture of Georgia Hale on the back cover and they thought it was me. The publisher made a mistake.

They kept the long shots, made at Truckee in the snow, because I was so far from the camera that they really couldn't tell the difference. I remember one night having dinner at a bridge table in front of the fireplace, and he was telling me what he was going to do in the scene the next day, a scene that he thought was going to be hilariously funny, and it wasn't funny to me. That left a lasting impression because I realised that when I went to the studio to see him perform the same scene he had told me about, it was very, very funny, in pantomime, when he acted it out. I remember looking at Charlie, on nights like that, in front of the fireplace He had marvellous eyes – beautiful, expressive eyes – but you always had the feeling that he wasn't looking at you, he was looking through you as if he was on another plane. It was in those moments that he was actually creating something – thinking about what he was going to do the next day. Like many Englishmen, he liked the same thing over and over and over. I've often wondered about that because the English are so brilliant and humorous, but Charlie could have six suits exactly the same. You opened the closet door and here was a row of shoes, all the same, high button suede top, black bottom all in a row. He loved to have breakfast in bed – the same thing for breakfast. Marmalade, toast, two soft-boiled eggs, coffee and so forth. Every day the same.

    He didn't comb his hair, because he always wanted the hair very bushy for the tramp character, very curly. He'd get on the grey suit he had so many of, and the high button shoes and he'd go down into the automobile. His chauffeur would drive him to the studio and when he would arrive Alf Reeves would shout, "He's here!" and that's the only time I ever heard that in the theatre, or on film sets. "He's here!" Like the prince has arrived, you know.

Other days, he'd send Kono (his chauffeur and valet), down to the studio or he'd call on the telephone and say, "Send everybody home, I don't feel funny today." He'd stay in bed and have his breakfast and he'd read the paper, and he'd have a favourite book that he was reading, and he'd talk about the philosophy of the writer. One thing I can remember he said was to be very careful how you analyse the word "intelligence" because there are may different kinds. I've thought about that many times because he certainly had a unique type of intelligence. In so many ways so great and in others so self-destructive.

When he'd stay home, he was extremely melancholy and temperamental and there were times when he'd get to the dinner table that night and be mad at the cook – and send the food back. He even fired the cook one time because a potato was too hard. He would take out his bad mood at home when he was disappointed by not being able to continue to create, and it just wouldn't come, so he'd just put it off until he did feel that he could create.

On good days he'd go out of the house whistling, very happy because he had thought of the way it should be done. He could do it.

We spoke to Jacqui in Bishop. Nellie O'Brien was 88, suffered from sciatica, but her memory was sharp and she talked well. However, her home was a caravan – a mobile home, as it was euphemistically known in America – and somewhat cramped for filming. Jacqui said she had the luck to arrive at the same time as her doctor, who considered the interview would do her good. So all was set for the following day; David took the precaution of chartering an aircraft. Meanwhile, we had two important interviews to complete first, one with veteran director King Vidor.

King Vidor

We were very close friends for about ten years. We were both tennis players, and I suppose our acquaintanceship started with Sunday afternoon tennis games. Then we had two yachts, about the same size, his was the *Panacea* and mine was the *Runaway*. We would anchor near each other at Catalina so we could exchange having the other for dinner.

It was very funny. I must have been at his house two or three times a week because whenever he had a prominent guest, like George Bernard Shaw or H.G. Wells or Alexander Woollcott, he would always want me to come over and help him tell Goldwyn stories. They were always entertained by the Goldwyn stories. So those that he couldn't remember, I would fill in. Chaplin acted all the scenes of his picture every night, whether at home or in Chasen's restaurant or the Brown Derby in Beverly Hills. He was acting all the scenes of his screenplays. He was trying them out on his friends and seeing how we reacted, how we laughed. I remember one time he was illustrating his sense of comedy, and he said that some comedians would be content to have a scene walking into a room, and have one gag in the scene. Charlie's approach was to have six gags, one on entering, one on closing the door, a couple as he crossed the room and two more gags opening the other door. That was his goal.

If he wanted to describe somebody he'd seen he could do the damnedest dialogue. I remember we were in the back of his automobile and he described a couple of trout fishermen he'd seen on a river someplace. There was a whole life – the names of the flies they had devised...They were all made up, but I remember we laughed so hard I finally got down on the floor in a cramped position to stop laughing. It showed that his ability to mimic included dialogue, just the same as pantomime.

And one time we'd been skiing up at Yosemite and coming back in a public bus was my wife and Paulette Goddard and Charlie. The rest of the bus was filled with people and Charlie started doing that language thing that he did in *The Great Dictator* – speaking German, without knowing how to speak German. It sounded like German, then it went into Chinese and Japanese. Finally I suggested, "How does French sound to a Japanese?" And that's terribly complicated. It went on for two or three hours without stopping in the bus going from Yosemite to Fresno, where we boarded a train. And the people were cheering and applauding, he was doing it for the entire bus. It was an unforgettable experience.

I thought him the greatest actor I ever knew, but I never thought he was a great director. I remember being on the set in London for *The Countess of Hong Kong* and he was directing Marlon Brando and Sophia Loren. I saw Brando had to play in a few moments. Brando was so puzzled – "I can't act like he does. How am I going to interpret this the same way?" Charlie was acting it out and one of the things of direction that I used to be particularly aware of was not acting it out for the actors but to convey it to them through words, what they should be thinking about, and bring out their own individuality and not have them copy.

When we became aware of camera movement, and the freedom of composition, he didn't use any of those techniques for years. He went on with the same style that he'd learned at Mack Sennett's – that was just straight on, and either full figure or closeup waist figure. The lighting was just smack-on straight lighting.

One day I was in his studio and he says, "Have you got my feet in?" And the cameraman said, "No." "Well, get them in." They just pulled everything back and they were ready to go in one minute. Well, our techniques, if you changed the composition, the lighting had to be completely changed. He was very sensitive about being corrected. I had tried it once or twice and he was terribly sensitive about my correcting him about anything. I would never say anything about a film.

He either closed his eyes and ears to what was happening or he figured that that was the right way for him and he was able to achieve much more emotion and story-telling in his own way. But it seemed to me old fashioned.

I made a film (in 1928) called *Show People*. Now, not many people have directed Chaplin outside of his own films, and I was glad of the opportunity to be able to have him in one of mine. It was a film with Marion Davies and I don't think he'd do that for anyone else. I was a friend, and Marion a good friend and the power of the Hearst press made him accept it. He was glad to do it. He had fun doing it and he took the direction. It was very simple, but he took direction.

He used to cut his own hair. I don't know why, it may go back to his early days when he didn't have enough money. But once he said after tennis – he used to call me Buddy – "Come on up, Buddy, and I'll give you a haircut." So I sat on a high stool and he gave me a haircut. A few weeks later I was down in Los Angeles and I went in the barber shop and the barber said, "Who cut your hair last time?" And quietly I said, "Charlie Chaplin." The barber looked at me and said, "I ask you a civil question. I expect a civil answer." Charlie said to me once, "Nobody outside the studio has ever seen the way that I turn a corner. They all think I go round on the inside foot, and I really turn a corner on the outside foot". What he meant was, it's like bicycle riding, or skating, you lean in and the weight goes on the inside foot. But he's doing it on the outside foot and that made it look humorous. He had an infinite sense of proper timing. He was not content to have just a few things, he would build and that's what made him such a genius, if I may use the word, these things all built until they became excruciatingly funny. That's one of the important things of filmmaking – to increase the emotion – and I know sometimes I used to try it and studio executives would come in and either cut it out or have me reshoot it. They were afraid of it. But Charlie's humour increased and increased.

The next interview was the most crucial of all. And we still had no idea whether we'd secure it. Georgia Hale had returned home, and had agreed to our coming round – to return the manuscript. So we had two alternatives; either we left the crew at the hotel, and telephoned them when and if we persuaded Georgia, or they came with us and hovered round the corner. David plumped for the second choice.

We walked up to that fateful door, and twisted the odd bell device. Georgia herself answered the door. She had the same grotesque outfit on, but we were so relieved to see her it didn't worry us. She was surprisingly welcoming.

"How is your sister?" asked David, with a thoughtfulness I lacked. (I just wanted to shriek "When can we bring the crew in?"). She said she was much better. She was glad to have the manuscript back, and very pleased by the appearance of a photocopy. "Well, for evermore," she said (her favourite expression).

I explained what a miserable two weeks she had put us through. She replied, with a sweep of those endless eyelashes, "Is this you?" She pointed to a clipping from the *Los Angeles Times*, our appeal for Chaplin veterans, and next to it was a list she had started with the names Lita Grey, Virginia Sherrill [sic].

"We've come 6,000 miles to see Georgia Hale," we said, backing the poor woman up against the wall. "We're doing this programme on Chaplin – using the out-takes – and you know what we've found? Yes, THE scene. Your scene from *City Lights*'. And we've come all this way to get an interview with you".

"An interview? What exactly would you want to do?"

"We would just want to film an interview with you."

We had spoken the word she had feared. "FILM!" She looked shocked. "Georgia, that's why the crew is waiting around the corner." We expected total collapse and hysteria. She blinked and then said, mildly, "Go on, bring them in, I don't mind."

We were so relieved we grabbed her in turn and kissed her energetically. As David went out to bring them in, I prepared her for the size of an English crew. The thing that worried her was the fact that she only had two wine glasses. "You have Herman to thank for this," she said. "I don't know what you said to him, but he just loves you two guys and he called me and said, 'I don't know what they want you for, but whatever it is they really need you. Why don't you come back for half a day?' I was way out in canyon country. I said, 'I'll send them a letter'. 'No', he said. 'I think you ought to come in.' So I finally said, 'Well, find out when they're leaving and make it their last day.' So he did."

Georgia Hale

They would always say "You're unusually beautiful. You could be a sensation. You could be in pictures, you could do anything you wanted to" and this was always being said to me, which was tormenting because I was poor and I couldn't get out of my surroundings. I had no money, and I couldn't help my mother and father, who needed help. But then one day I went to the movies and saw this little character, Charlie Chaplin, who was as down as anybody could be, he had nothing. I saw him depict the great fact that no matter how low you were, if you have a spirit within you that can pick yourself up when the world knocks you down – if you have that kind of spirit then you can be anything. If I could emulate him and be hopeful and courageous no matter what happened to me, or how many blows I had to take, I could attain anything I set my heart on. I could be what I wanted to be and rise above poverty and bless my mother and father, which was really my motive.

My first meeting with Charlie was at the FBO studios and it was there that *The Salvation Hunters* was going to be shown to Charlie and Nazimova. I was seated in front of them and I could hear all the wonderful things he was saying about this picture, and he mentioned me, too. That I was "outstanding". And when the lights went on, everybody ran to the group around him, and I stood aside. He asked, "By chance, is the leading lady here?" And they said, "Oh yes, she's right over there." He came over and he took my hand in both of his and he said, "You know, you did a beautiful job and I predict great things in the future for you." In a moment or two Josef von Sternberg came over and said, "Would you be offended if I don't take you home? There's a couple here from Vienna and they've asked me to take them home." Charlie overheard this and said, "Why,

I'd be delighted to drive you home." On the way, he asked if I'd like to have some tea. So we went to a little tiny place and I just sat there amazed that I was sitting opposite Charlie Chaplin, the man I had adored since I was six. I sat opposite him and watched him eat and drink his tea; everything that Charlie did was so dainty and so beautifully done, and it had such rhythm to it, that you were fascinated. Everything was like a dance, it was like the ballet. The man I imagine could have been a ballet artist. Then he went to pay the bill and he searched in one pocket and then another and he didn't have a dime and he was so embarrassed. I paid the bill and I was so delighted that he didn't have any money, because then he was indebted to me and I felt that in some way he'll get in touch to pay me back.

He took a lot of tests of a lot of girls, among which was Carol Lombard. I saw the shots of them the following day with him – they were all marvellous, I thought. And I thought I was perfectly terrible. "Everyone was marvellous, but me," I said. "No," he said. "You are outstanding and you've got the part."

But Charlie raved about me to Douglas Fairbanks, who signed me for a year's contract with an option for five years. Charlie was amazed. He didn't dream that his dear friend was going to sign me. But Doug didn't know that he shouldn't have done it. He thought Charlie had Lita Grey and that it was all set. But Charlie in the meantime had made up his mind the moment he saw *Salvation Hunters*, that he was going to have me for his leading lady. He even went so far as to say "That is my future wife" in his mind. Immediately Doug apologised and released me and I was under contract then to Chaplin and Lita Grey was taken out of the picture and the whole thing was remade with me in it.

Charlie thought I was looking for the dancehall girl to be a flighty, flirtatious individual and all the girls in the tests were that type. I looked miserable compared to the other girls, and I thought surely he'd want the vivacious type, but he didn't. He was looking for that sad, sullen dancehall girl. That's why he wanted me.

When I did the dancehall girl I always had my hands on my hips which was not what he directed at all. But that was exactly what he wanted – this girl, defiant and cold and solemn. If I forgot to do it, he would say, "No, put your hands on your hips." And another time, when I'm making an exit, I throw my hand in the air. He says, "Leave that in". There were many little things that if they were real and true and you felt it, he was tickled to get the right, natural reaction.

If a scene wasn't going well, he had that wonderful sense of never criticising you or beating you down. He always used the word "dear". "Now, dear, let's try it this way." And that word would give you such a renewed sense that you could do it. Maybe with some people he would use a different method, but with me, he knew I'd be beaten down very quickly and he always used gentle encouragement.

He knew that one big fault of actors was overacting and he knew that hamming a thing meant that it didn't have the proper action behind it – they had lost the action for the motions. So after he gave you the scene, he'd always say – even if it was a deep, emotional scene, just before the camera would go, he'd say, "Now do this scene poorly, walk through it." And then he would get it, because nobody was hamming it, nobody was overdoing it, they were really feeling it, just by those words, "Do it poorly."

If he wasn't inspired, he'd come on the set with his hands stuffed in his pants pockets, his shoulders folded together and a scowl on his face and he wouldn't do a thing. He would let all the people wait – wouldn't matter how many were being paid or how much it cost – and after he'd sat there in a daze for hours, he would leave and call it off for the day and then he wouldn't call us back for a week until he was inspired again.

One time Harry d'Arrast said that we'd shoot (the next day) only if the sun was shining. So when I got up and it was raining, I knew there would be no work. But I was the only one who seemed to interpret it that way because everybody was there but me. Finally the phone rang and they said, "Why aren't you on the set?" Well, I almost went to pieces. I slapped on a horrible makeup and threw on my clothes and went over there and I was such a mess they warned me not to go near Charlie – just to stay away from him until he'd cooled down. So I never went near him. I sat far away and wouldn't even look in his direction. Finally he sent Harry d'Arrast over to me and said, "Go and tell her to put on a decent makeup." That was the first communication I had from him, and then finally he warmed up to me and I was forgiven.

He thought I was taking advantage of him. He said, "The only reason you do this is because you know I like you very much. Now that you've found out, you're going to take advantage of me." And this hurt more than anything else he could have said because I didn't do it to hurt him or anybody and I told him that. And he believed me.

There was a woman on the set who was so afraid of Charlie, and keeping her little job there, that she was afraid to go to the ladies room, even though she was in desperate need of going. So she came to me and told me about how frightened she was of him and that she couldn't leave the set. And I said, "Now, you can go and I'll tell Mr Chaplin and don't worry, he won't fire you because I'll explain." And she went and I did explain to Mr Chaplin and he said, "Oh, I wouldn't do that to anyone, I'm so sorry I gave that impression." Because Charlie was very sensitive, he'd never really wanted to hurt anybody. In fact, one time when he did brush aside somebody coming into the studio and didn't autograph their little piece of paper, he couldn't work, he was so upset that he had offended this little person.

Edna Purviance worked with Charlie for years and she evidently didn't have much talent for acting, but Charlie always drummed everything into her and showed her how to do it, walked through the part, and finally did get each scene out of her. One day she couldn't do the scene as usual and his patience came to an end and he called her every dirty name he could think of and spoke to her terribly. And she, who always took this chastisement without making a nudge about it, got into a rage – a rage of a tigress – and she came after him. She was going to kill him, he said, and he saw the expression in her face and he got so frightened he ran for his life – with her after him. He shut himself in his little studio and locked the door and wouldn't come out. Edna finally went to her room, calmed down and it was over and she was back to her own sweet self again. And then Charlie gradually peeked out his door and tiptoed down the steps of his little cottage and over to her room and gently tapped at the door and softly said "Edna". Edna opened the door and forgave him and they were back together again. I really think he could make anyone do a scene. He did it – he felt it – himself. He acted the scene out for you, including every flicker of the eye. He just felt it, gave it to you and instilled it into you so that you just had to give a terrific performance.

Sometimes he was effeminate and delicate and then again he could be very nasty and frown. On the other hand, he would put his hand above his head and act like a tiny little baby. He would do all these things to get you to react the way he wanted you to. Everything he did with a purpose, when he was directing. He was one hundred per cent absorbed in his directing, and he didn't care how long it took, or how many retakes he took. He didn't care how much money he spent. When it came to pictures, if it took five years, he wanted it as perfect as he could get it. That never bothered me, because I knew he was a perfectionist and I knew he was seeing things that nobody else saw and wanting things that nobody else even knew could be in the picture. And so with this infinite faith I had in his genius, my patience was as infinite with his retakes and retakes.

The first scene I shot in *The Gold Rush* was the scene where the sledge comes down the icebank towards the cabin and the girls come face to face with the little tramp, and they laugh and throw snowballs and he's standing there, taking it all in.

The studio snow came from the Union Ice Company, which was only a block away and they would haul in the shavings from the blocks of ice in trucks, and then pour it over the slopes. The false snow covered a white painted background of wood, covered in canvas.

The scene where I slapped the leading man (Malcolm Waite) – that was the real McCoy. The scene called for him to take me in his arms and give me a good big kiss and Charlie kept retaking it, because he always retook everything to get the right reaction from me, and finally I was in a rage and I really slapped him awfully hard across the face and that was the take that Charlie really wanted – the violent temper that came out when he kissed me once too often.

In *The Gold Rush* he seemed so delighted – I shouldn't really say this – but he seemed so delighted with me in the part and he voiced it – "At last I've got somebody that can do it, can act, can feel." There was no scene that I can remember where he didn't feel overjoyed at the way it was acted. The little shack that he worked in was really the first time I was ever alone with him, although it meant nothing. Because he invited me into it one time to talk over a scene. It was bare, it was wood and the wall was unpainted – a terrible looking unpainted desk and awful looking chairs and no rug, nothing. He saw that amazed look on my face, because I thought it would naturally be beautiful, since he was a millionaire after all. And he said, "You're amazed because it's so plain in here, aren't you? I wanted it plain, so I can think. I don't want to see things and have my thoughts go to what I'm seeing. I want to think within myself. If I had my way, I'd just have big black square walls put around the place where I couldn't see a thing."

I watched the Dance of the Rolls because I was seated right next to him, at the table. The girls at the New Year's Eve party were actually there, even though he was just dreaming it, supposedly, in the story. There was music played for it, and not only was there music played for it, but he sang (hummed). He made his own little noise, not actually a song but like little beats, so it would have a perfect tempo. It was a surprise to everyone. The actors, the electricians, everybody – and I still don't know whether Charlie did it inspirationally, spontaneously, or whether he had worked it out. All any of us knew was that he just sat down there and out of the air came this beautiful little dance. When he'd finished, everyone in the studio applauded.

The last scene was really the first time that Charlie could ever express anything toward me that was really legitimate, because for me he really belonged to Lita Grey. So there was absolutely a wall between us. We were very impersonal. But during the scene he had a legitimate chance to express what he evidently had been feeling, and that was an affection for me, so when he had a chance to kiss me, then the kiss lasted way longer than it should have lasted. And then he kept retaking it and retaking it, so then I was commencing to know that his feeling for me was more than just a director's for a leading lady, and of course I knew what my feeling was – all my life.

At every party that he did – with Beatrice Lillie or someone – he did great scenes, just extemporaneously. Why, he would perform things that if they could only have been shot, I tell you, they were so great. Some of the things he did alone and with others, I really think they were greater than the things that were photographed. He was so entertaining, whatever part he played, he was the whole show. And he always put on a show: real generous. He could make anybody act, and he did. He would take people who had no talent at all, or even any desire, really. Virginia Cherrill I really don't think had a desire to be an actress. She was a society girl; she just happened into it.

She was cast in the part (in *City Lights*) in the beginning, but she was not really an actress and he simply fought all the way to get her to do the scenes and never felt that he was getting them. But when it came to the final scene, the dramatic scene where she realises that after she has her sight, he was the one who was her benefactor, and she feels his hand and realises this is the chap that did all these things for her. She looks at him and the tears are supposed to roll down her eyes and the whole scene is the most dramatic scene in it. She couldn't do it. She simply couldn't do it. So he did reshoot that scene with me – that one dramatic scene that he simply couldn't get. And he got the most satisfying scene to himself.

And that night we went to the Double Eagle restaurant and he said, "I'm going to redo all *City Lights* with you, just the way I did *The Gold Rush*." And I was overjoyed because I loved that story and I knew I could have done that part so well, and then the whole thing was reversed.

Out of a clear sky he comes back to me and calls me over to the studio and he tells me off in the most vicious manner that I'm not going to do *City Lights* and to get it out of my mind and that it was all a mistake. I just cried and cried because I couldn't understand. Then a week or two passes and he calls me again and apologises. He said his publicity man had come to him and poisoned his mind against me. He told him that I was going to sue him if I didn't play that part and he believed him – and he says, "How I ever believed it I'll never know". And then he just simply got down on his knees and asked forgiveness. But in the meantime, they had shot the picture and instead of giving the big scene to her, he gave it to himself. It would have cost millions of dollars, naturally, to remake it and they all convinced him. It was finished anyway, and he said, "I'm going to sew it up the way it is."

But I can remember how I felt the scene. I could just feel what this blind girl felt toward her benefactor. She felt the hand of this chap, and realised that this was her friend and tears of joy burst out of her eyes – tears of joy at finding the one she had been wanting to find all this time, since she could see. Her desire to find the one who had done this for her was fulfilled. The scene was mine – I had it – he knew it, and he loved it and couldn't get over how happy he was. He couldn't wait to take me to dinner to tell me that it was all mine. But fate stepped in.

He didn't feel right about *City Lights*. He didn't feel – nor do I feel – that he got what he could have got into *City Lights*, although the whole world thought it was just beautiful. I never felt the thing was played the way it could have been played.

For the opening night, he invited (Albert) Einstein and his wife and me to go with him. All the way down, he kept saying, "I don't care if it's a failure or a success. What is fame? I don't care a bit about fame or being popular or accepted." And he kept on, convincing himself that he just didn't care how the evening went. At the end of the picture they all stood in acclamation, the theatre reverberated with the noise, whistling and everything, and then he admitted, like a little baby, "I do love the public, I've got to have acclaim. I've got to be accepted by people." He was himself; he admitted that he needed the applause of the world. He lived on it. He loved it. He said the same thing about the night of the Oscar, by the way (in 1972). When I was having lunch with him, he said that he didn't care, he didn't really know why he came over here. At the theatre that night, he was speechless with joy at the way people accepted him.

Early on the morning of Sunday, March 29th 1981, we went to the Santa Monica airport, where we clambered aboard a Cessna aircraft. The flight was uneventful except for a stomach-churning drop of 100 feet over the mountains. A woman travelling with us informed us that the local name for the outfit was "White Knuckle Airways".

At Bishop, Jacqui awaited us as we stepped out into the hot sunshine and pure air. We left the crew at the Copper Kettle Restaurant while we reconnoitred the trailer camp. Jacqui noticed that the curtains were drawn on Mrs O'Brien's home, so we beat a tactical retreat. "She is very wizened," said Jacqui, "and has a scar on her cheek about the size of a quarter, but she talks well."

We had lunch and set out to return at the appointed hour of 1.00pm. Just before we left, I heard a phrase in my head. "She won't speak to you." I was about to make a crack about it to David, but I'd been so pessimistic for so long I thought I'd forget it now.

We drove to the trailer park, and there was Jacqui. "At least she's smiling," said David, ever the optimist. But it must have been the sun in her eyes. She came to the window and said, "She won't speak to you."

I'm not superstitious, but two outstanding *coups* in two days just doesn't happen, so I was not all that surprised. We got out of our cars and wandered around, as though Nellie might see how many people had come from England to interview her – and relent. But only a hostile neighbour emerged from the caravan marked N.B. O'BRIEN, told us to go away and crossed to her own.

We reluctantly returned to the Copper Kettle, where Jacqui called the doctor, who seemed to shrug the event off. "She always makes alarmist calls," he said. "Come now or I'll be dead." But he could offer no grain of comfort. Our only course was to return to Los Angeles. And there was no chance of coming back, for we were due in New York the next day.

Oddly enough, another important lost figure telephoned me at the hotel – Alice White. She had worked at the studio – in her summer vacation she was script girl on von Sternberg's *The Sea Gull*. Chaplin had nicknamed her Peter Rabbit. The stills cameraman on *The Sea Gull* took some pictures of her which led directly to her becoming a star. But she was even more of a recluse than Nellie, so there was no chance of an interview. (She pretended she was going on a long trip.)

In New York, we spoke to Douglas Fairbanks Jr., who recalled what a great encourager Chaplin had been. "When I was on the stage, as a boy, my father came backstage briefly to say hello. Charlie talked until two in the morning. He talked of his sense of pure cinema, although his idea of technique remained static.

"He hated the idea of previews. For one thing, he was very mean, and he didn't like the idea of 1500 people seeing his work for nothing. My father and Sid Grauman decided to play a gag on him. They convinced him to have a small preview, with 150 people scientifically selected as a cross-section of a regular audience. They held it in a private theatre. Charlie said, 'What's the point? As soon as they see me, they'll know what to expect, and they'll laugh because they'll think they have to laugh.' 'Not at all,' said my father. 'They won't recognise you out of makeup, and anyway, you stay in the projection room and come out and stand at the back when the picture begins. No one will see you.'

"So that's what happened. Charlie was terribly nervous. He had taken a year over the picture. And he came and stood at the back, with clammy palms...and there wasn't a laugh from start to finish. He was in a terrible state. Not a chuckle. They just sat there. And what my father and Grauman had done was to bring in 150 wax dummies and dress them up."

Robert Parrish, an Oscar winning editor and for many years a director, was one of the pea-shooting kids in *City Lights*. He told us how Chaplin was "a dervish" – showing Virginia Cherrill how to do her part, skipping over the street and playing everyone else's part.

"He showed us what to do – he directed us by being us. He always seemed sorry to give the parts back to the people hired to play them. There was a reluctance that he couldn't be behind the camera and in front of it at the same time. I was invited years later to see the rushes on *Monsieur Verdoux* and there were four takes. It was just Charlie at the bottom of some stairs and he did a little sort of dance and went up the stairs and that was all there was to it. He said, 'Now tell me which of these you like the best.' The first two were fine and the fourth was fine but in the third the camera had panned momentarily off the set to show an electrician with his hand on a light. So I said 'I guess the first two or the fourth.' 'What was wrong with the third one?' 'Well, you can see the electrician.' 'What are you watching him for?' he said. 'You're supposed to be watching me.' I never knew quite whether he was joking. I don't think he was.'"

Our last interview was with Alistair Cooke, who came straight from delivering one of his BBC *Letters from America*. He was witty, analytical and anecdotal and he seemed to know precisely where to stop at the end of each 400-foot roll.

Alistair Cooke

I was doing a series of interviews for The *Observer* in 1933 when I was moving over from Yale to Harvard on a Fellowship and had the summer free, and was going out to the Coast. So of course I was excited and wrote off to all these people – Lubitsch, C. Aubrey Smith – and Chaplin. The interesting thing is that the personal letter that came back was from Chaplin, and it was partly because when he'd been in England two years before he'd met the Astors, so The *Observer* was a connection. I went to his studio and met him and the idea was an hour's interview, but he showed me round the *City Lights* set, the ruins of the statue and the Embankment and all that, then he took me to lunch. I left about midnight and then spent the entire summer with him. I was at Harvard in the interim, but the following summer he wrote to me and said he'd got this idea to make a film about Napoleon on St Helena, and would I do the script with him? I was, of course, enormously excited and flattered, so I went out to work with him and did so through the summer.

Chaplin was very easygoing when he wasn't working. But when I arrived to work on this Napoleon idea, he was quite a different character in the sense that he was so disciplined.

We would be at the studio at ten o'clock – Carter De Haven, an old vaudeville man, and old Henry Bergman. His function was simply to sit there. Chaplin would strut up and down being Napoleon and then he would turn to Henry Bergman and say, "Okay, Henry?" And Bergman sat there like a French farmer who had two words and he would sigh and say, "Mmm. I'd say, yeah, yeah. It was very good." That was all. That was his entire function, but it worked because Chaplin trusted his instinct. It was rather nice having a sort of lay producer – a fly on the wall and you just looked up and said, "All right?" "Yeah."

We worked every day in this little room, this miserable little room, which was a big shock. Mind you, the studio itself was nothing remotely like as pretentious as I'd imagined. It had this pebbledash sort of stucco with imitation Elizabethan beams on the outside. It looked like what would now be a very third rate cafe. This particular room had peeling wallpaper, a terribly worn carpet, an upright piano about eighty years old and terribly out of tune and a trestle table with a couple of ashtrays – in those days Chaplin smoked – and bentwood chairs. There isn't a movie company, however modest, making three minute documentaries that has such a humble office. He said he wasn't at ease working in comfortable surroundings. He always suspected not so much his success, as the monetary rewards, and it's one reason he wouldn't handle money. He was comfortable in the kind of shabby surroundings he'd known as a vaudevillian.

I'd go to the library and come back with the memoirs of somebody who was with Napoleon at St Helena and he got very warmed up about this thing. It was beginning to take shape and he was very excited at playing for the first time a dramatic part.

I remember him coming in one morning, very cheerful, we were going to play tennis, and he said, "You know, about this Napoleon thing. It's all right for somebody else – they want to see the little man. So maybe some other time." And he never mentioned it again.

I now think that this was his way of going into sound, but not with the little man. And I think his instinct was correct there, to do this dramatic film where Charles Chaplin, not Charlie Chaplin, would appear as Napoleon, and so it would be a complete break and maybe his misgivings about that were the reasons for his saying, "It's all right for somebody else." I was sort of strung there, being paid the colossal sum of $100 a week, which was marvellous in the

Depression, and thought, "Now what do I do?" But he was very nice about it. He then got other ideas. He was going to do a revue, a film with six episodes, and the most bizarre was to be the crucifixion done as a night club scene, a very sort of Hollywood thing, all these rich, flashy people applauding. It was a very good idea but of course it would have been impossible in those days. And he mimed the whole thing. And then the same thing. "Well, maybe for Aldous Huxley, but not for me." Everybody who worked with Chaplin told me that it was very exciting in the beginning because Chaplin was totally absorbed with any movie he was making and his absorption was at the expense of everybody else's life. He was marvellous with them when things were going well. When they weren't going well, he would decide to forget dinner, and you'd better forget dinner. If there was some important person appearing in Hollywood, he wouldn't show up and nobody could telephone him. They also told me when you came to a crisis, where he couldn't see how something was going to work, then he was murderous on anybody who wanted time off or who interfered in any way.

The crisis I know about is *City Lights*. He told me that he went on for days. He wanted to introduce the tramp to the flower girl and there were several problems. The first was how should he know she was blind. Second problem was he had an idea that he, the little tramp, with no money whatsoever, should pay for some flowers and not get his change back because – its a typical bit of Chaplin pathos – then he would look forlorn and realise that he didn't want to hurt this girl. So he worked on this and the recognition of the blindness was easy. He picked Virginia Cherrill because he said she looked blind anyway. Now apparently they tried all kinds of variations to get across the notion that he has no money – and to get across to her that she keep the change.

He woke up one morning, he said, and it suddenly occurred to him – the slamming door of an automobile. So what happens is that he goes to the girl (walking through the rich man's limousine to avoid a cop),[30] says he'd like a flower, gives her everything he has in the world, which could well be a dollar or a dime, and as she's reaching for the change (she drops the coin and that's how he knows she's blind) she hears the rich man walk back across the sidewalk, get in the car, slam the door, and the car takes off. She's about to give the change and she says, "Oh, thank you, sir," and Chaplin looks at her and realises what's happened and turns round and tiptoes away without his change. Well, it's just like water running over a pebble in the film. But whenever I see it, I still wince a little at the thought of all the people whose private lives were devastated by his working out of this simple trick.

In 1932 he'd been to Bali, in the Pacific, and he had learned from these girls the art of Balinese dancing, and he'd taken films of their dancing and then his doing it, which was marvellous – absolutely perfect choreography. When he was talking about this trip, he said, "I'd like to show you the film of it." It was now eleven pm. He picks up the telephone and calls his projectionist, who's at home of course, gone to bed. He storms at this man – "Get in your car and

---

30. The gag can be seen in *The Idle Class*; the tramp walks through a limousine into a fancy dress party, and his clothes are assumed by the the doorman to be fancy dress.

come over here!" – so about midnight the man arrives sulkily, sleepily, and we see the film. When it's over, Charlie goes out, thanks him profusely and the man goes home. Then Chaplin sat down and he began to chuckle and he said, "You know, this could be very funny in a movie. You see, this fellow is just married. They've just got into the house and it's about nine o'clock in the evening, and the fellow goes "Oh, darling, aren't you tired?" And he did all this, mimicked the wife being coy and then the fellow dashing to the bedroom and using all kinds of lotions and perfumes. He acted the whole thing out and then the man gets in bed and the telephone rings and at the other end of the phone is this monster saying, "What are you doing there? Get over here at once!" And then he roared with laughter and that was the way of dissipating all his guilt. I mean, I was quite shocked at the way things happened, but when the man had gone he went into this fantasy and of course you could forgive him anything because he was such a marvellous scoundrel of a performer.

16. Inching Forward

We spent our days back at Teddington watching the rushes, a dispiriting experience at the best of times. Nonstop interviews are not cinematic and watching them on the big screen makes you long to do something with the material. It also makes you acutely aware of the ill-formed question and the uninformative answer.

David and I began to refresh our memories by viewing the earliest Chaplin films, the Essanays and the Keystones. We were amazed at how awful they looked. It wasn't just that the prints were of bad quality – which they invariably were – the films themselves were so crude and obvious one could hardly raise a smile. Small wonder that Chaplin's reputation had suffered when these one and two-reelers were all that people saw on television with jarring music tracks. Nothing dates quicker than humour. A radio show you adored twenty years ago will generally embarrass you today. The reason is that anything successful is instantly copied, elaborated, improved upon and the 'improvers' walk all over the original idea until there is precious little left. The Keystones and the Essanays were simple and joyous, much loved and highly successful. But their gags have been recycled so often that the originals appear lifeless. The later films suffered less because they were less easy to copy, the gags being more idiosyncratic than the kicks up the rear which seemed to be the sole trademark of Keystones.

It was a great boost to our morale to show something like *Modern Times* (not that there is *anything* like *Modern Times*!) – a silent film made in the mid-thirties, which I had not seen for many years, and which became at once my favourite Chaplin.

But faced with a surfeit of Keystones which could only be described as dried-up, and a handful of Essanays, which were only marginally more watchable, how were we ever going to produce a programme which did justice to this period? The answer became increasingly obvious – forget them.

During our sojourn in California, David Shepard, the former archivist now working for the Directors' Guild, told me that some Chaplin footage had been discovered in Kansas City, Missouri, by an academic, Douglas C. Moore, professor of film history at the University of Missouri.

I contacted him at once, and was amazed by his description of the film. It had been taken, as an amateur film, by Ralph Barton, a friend of Chaplin from the 1920s. Barton, an artist on *Vanity Fair*, had illustrated Anita Loos' *Gentlemen Prefer Blondes*, and Anita Loos played the part of Camille in an amateur film made by Barton, while every conceivable artist at large in the United States appeared in cameo roles.

Unfortunately, the professor's pet subject appeared to be copyright. Having been approached by a man called Karl Klein, a nephew of Barton's who was anxious to donate his film to the nation, he then proceeded to frighten him away with talk of copyright.

I offered to restore the original and save a print made for him as well as for Klein, and to return the original to Klein, so that he could donate it to the AFI, but I got nowhere. Fortunately, the professor eventually parted with Klein's address. Thus began a series of negotiations which spread over months.

Once collectors and film agencies heard that we were working on a Chaplin series, we were offered documentaries and compilation films which were said to contain rarities, but which seldom did.

Philip Jenkinson ran a company called Filmfinders. He had the largest collection of films in private hands in the country, and he had more than twenty years experience in hunting for rare material. We asked him about a fragment referred to occasionally by historians: a rehearsal scene from *City Lights* in which Chaplin plays the scene in which he examines a nude statue in a shop window scene in ordinary clothes. To our amazement he found it.

The Museum of Modern Art sent us the long-awaited *Spanish People at Pickfair* roll, which turned out to be a 35mm reel of excellent quality but of baffling content. It contained the scene shown in Laurence Irving's snapshot of Chaplin with the globe and the German *Pickelhaube*. Chaplin appears, wearing Pickford's costume from *Pollyanna*, as a ballet dancer. In one shot he knocks himself out with boxing gloves. In another, he shuffles across the lawn, doing his famous walk in bedroom slippers.

I had an idea the tall man in the group might be Laurence Irving. I sent him a frame enlargement. "Yes, indeed," he replied, "I remember those Spanish visitors, but had forgotten they were at Pickfair on that Sunday jollification. They were not royal, but Douglas, in entertaining them, was fulfilling his obligation to their monarch. Before he came to London and bore me off to Hollywood, he and Mary had been to Spain and were invited to an audience with Luis Alfonso. The first words he spoke to them after greeting them were, 'Well, Douglas, how is Fatty Arbuckle?'

"Douglas was deeply touched at the King's concern for this famous comic who had been unjustly and viciously humiliated by the hypocritical tycoons of the industry and the Hearst press. 'May I, Sir, tell him of your inquiry after him?' In due course he did so and did much to restore Fatty's morale. So when these Spanish people turned up and introduced themselves as leaders of the Spanish film industry (whatever that may have been at the time) Douglas treated them as honoured guests. He and all of us at the studio soon regretted this, for they proved to be garrulous and arrogant bores. As later I found when, now and again, to help the British Council, I lectured to theatrical or film folk from Europe, I soon discovered that they impatiently awaited the end of my discourse in order to talk about themselves. So it was with those Spaniards in Hollywood."

17. If Walls Could Speak

To a film historian, there is only one place as exciting as a film vault, and that is a cellar full of rare documents. David Robinson had told us about *les caves* at Vevey, and we were dismayed not to have seen them on our first visit.

Our return trip, however, was organised purely for this purpose. Rachel explained that there had been a fire at Le Manoir (we momentarily paled) which had slightly damaged Oona's bedroom. We would stay in nearby Corseau, at the Hotel Chatonneyre, and be picked up at 9.30 each morning.

The journey to Le Manoir took a mere three minutes. Rachel guided us down stone steps and into the former wine cellars. She equipped us with white coats and showed us our particular cellar. It was large, lit by neon, and lined with thirteen wooden cupboards. The same key opened all of them. The press books were beautifully wrapped in brown paper and marked, the stills were in cardboard or wooden boxes. The only drawback to the place was the damp – it was coming through the carpets, had affected the cupboards and was eating into the press books on the lower shelves. The underside of some of them was green. However, the pages, although fragile, were surviving.

We started with stills, tracking down positives and being amazed at how much unusual and fascinating material had been left out of Chaplin's *My Life in Pictures*.

One box came from the Sydney Chaplin collection. This contained the earliest and most historic material – including a postcard sent by Charlie from Tijuana, Mexico, in 1911 to his cousin Aubrey Chaplin at his pub in London. Rachel pointed out how bad Chaplin's writing was at this period, not to mention his spelling. One card showed the Karno plumbers' sketch, and Chaplin had scrawled "plummers" on the front, but got someone else to write the address in a more elegant hand. These fragments of Chaplin's early life were very touching. One tends to forget, with the memory of the urbane author-actor-director-composer, that he had only two years of schooling. And one overlooks the phenomenal effort of self-education that helped to transform the Cockney urchin into the most famous man in the world.

Chaplin had some splendid portraits made in Minneapolis and several pictures showed him posing in front of posters for *A Night in an English Music Hall*.

The Keystone period was covered in hindsight, and not too well. The most revelatory part was the first wave of worldwide fame during the war, with stories of what Chaplin's films meant to the troops and the people at home. A few of the most elaborate fan letters were included – Chaplin got 53,000 on his 1921 London trip – including a poem painted and illuminated with great care. The poem was awful – 'He's an awfully little chap (lin) And I don't care a rap (lin)' – but the painting was charming.

There were eight colossal press books covering the Mutual period, even though it lasted only eighteen months. Lettered in gold on the front THE BOOK OF CHAPLIN, they were beautifully hand-lettered inside by Mutual's president John Freuler.

The later press books appear to have been supervised by Alf Reeves, and presumably Nelly Bly Baker had the task of sticking the clippings in. Certainly, everything was put in, both brickbats and bouquets. The clipping service was so assiduous that even if someone refers to Chaplin in a 2,000-word article about truck gardening, in it went. This made me suspect Chaplin did not examine them closely, because he would soon have stopped that. One of the first items I read concerned a temporary injunction secured by Chaplin in 1921 against the Sales Corporation and Ralph Spence, who was making "new" Chaplin films from so-called "surplus scraps". These turned out to be 750,000 feet of Mutual out-takes![32]

This explained how Chaplin came to own the material. He would not have been able to depart from Mutual with all his out-takes. Nor had he any legal grounds to stop the Sales Corporation from exploiting them, any more than he had against Essanay when they added an extra reel to *Burlesque on Carmen*. But if he made them an offer they could not refuse, he could stop the new films being made and acquire the

---

32. The fact that Spence was making a film called *The Bootlegger* suggests he had a lot of *The Cure* (*The World Magazine*, December 11, 1921). Spence later became one of the industry's leading title-writers, and worked on the dialogue for Keaton's talkies at MGM. The author of the play *The Gorilla*, he also became a friend of Keaton's.

material into the bargain. The clipping albums contained newspaper photographs with captions explaining who some of our mysterious visitors were. The mysterious "Bishop", in British army uniform, whom I had assumed to be a Colonel Bishop, turned out to be the Bishop of Birmingham, Rt. Rev. Henry Russell Wakefield, who had close links with the British film industry. He was chairman in 1917 of the Cinema Commission of Inquiry, instituted by the National Council of Public Morals, a committee which consisted of people such as Marie Stopes and Baden-Powell.[33] He was also connected to the Territorial Army, hence the uniform.

The socialist Max Eastman was described by Chaplin in the *St Louis Star*[34] as "one of my best friends. He is a radical, poet and the editor of *The Liberator*. A charming and sympathetic fellow who thinks. All of his doctrines I do not subscribe to but that makes no difference to our friendship."

The Harry Lauder visit occurred while Chaplin was trying to make *A Dog's Life* in 1918. The visit was responsible for the film being postponed three times. Chaplin gave Lauder $1,000 for the British Wounded Soldiers' Fund, and it was he who suggested making the film. In doing so, he risked a violation of his First National contract, but evidently First National realised it would be counter-productive to sue over a charitable cause. Besides, the United States was now Britain's ally in the war.

Chaplin's conduct in the war created almost as much controversy as his alleged left-wing connections later on. Many people felt that he should have returned to England and joined the army, for he was still a British citizen. It was not enough that he did far more valuable work for the morale of troops and civilians by making his films. It was not enough that he sold thousands more Liberty Bonds than any politician. They wanted no exceptions. A letter from Chaplin to a friend, Lt. Clive Fenn, was reprinted in *Fall In*, the organ of the Middlesex Territorial Regiment:

> I would that I were at the front, as you so strikingly put it "drilling a squad" with, as you add "a kick from that wonderful foot of mine".

33. *Films & Filming*, April 1983, p.25.

34. December 11, 1921, p.6c.

"Wonderful foot" if you will – but with a staunch heart too, if I were there. Those of you who have set the proper pace – I would try to meet it. I am sorry that my professional demands do not permit my presence in the Mother Country; I hope that in so saying I do not sound coldblooded or hiding behind my player's coat. There are some of us who cannot be at the front and there are many of you – London men and all – who can be. We cheer you for your spirit and your courage and the cheerful way you are each doing "your little bit". If, in my modest way, in occasional bits of cheery nonsense as "Charlie Chaplin" of the films I can instil a moment of brief relief from the brunt of the fray, this is my contribution to the man at the front.

Had Chaplin joined the army at the outbreak of war, in August 1914, he would today be no more than a footnote in film history. For he stood a very slim chance of surviving, and had he been killed he would have been remembered only for a handful of Keystone comedies, none of which had any lasting merit. Many other potentially great artists were killed, but in this case we know what we would have lost – in itself a great argument for pacifism! There were volumes of newsprint testifying to the remarkable effect on morale of Chaplin's films. A photo from *The Sphere* showed soldiers and nurses around a ward screen, on which hangs a painting of Chaplin, and another showing soldiers painting Chaplin figures on plates: "Christmas in the Hospitals".

A cartoon was headed HORRIBLE POSSIBILITY; a soldier talks to a civilian:

"It was dreadful for us when Lord Kitchener died."

"I dunno. It mighter been Charlie Chaplin."

St Paul Pioneer, March 25 1917: "Sir John French orders troops to stop growing the Chaplin mustache as it subverts the dignity of His Majesty's troops in the field."

I had always understood that Chaplin was unknown in Germany during the war, and Chaplin himself confirmed this when he described

Chaplin as German officer already suggests *The Great Dictator*; a scene from *Shoulder Arms* (1918), with Edna Purviance and Syd Chaplin

his visit to Berlin in 1921 and only one man – a former prisoner-of-war – recognised him.

The press clipping book contradicts this. The Germans at Ypres called the London-Scottish regiments "Chaplins", the films "having as great a vogue on the Berlinstrasse as in Piccadilly". Certainly American films were still reaching Germany in 1915, although in greatly reduced numbers due to the British blockade.

The most surprising revelation was from the *Macon (Georgia) News* February 9 1918, which said that in practically every enemy submarine brought to port, in every German trench, were drawings or statuettes of Chaplin, labelled satirically "America's national hero". The idea originated with Germans who left America at the outbreak of war and joined the German army.

The press books even had an explanation of Chaplin's moustache (not quite as extraordinary as the explanation of Hitler's moustache, given by the former chauffeur to Mussolini, now living in Los Angeles: "Of course it was based on Chaplin's. He wanted to be loved. Everyone knows that."). Chaplin was reported to have said, "You may not believe it, but I wear this moustache because I think I am a better looking man with it than without it."[35] *The Reading (Pennsylvania) Telegram*, November 19, 1916, in an editorial, declared that the moustache was intended as a caricature of young Americans. Americans travelling abroad saw only waiters and valets without moustaches and they quickly grew one, saying,"I don't want to be taken for a waiter over there."

On the other hand, George French, an English music hall artist, claimed that Chaplin took the moustache from him, and he had a picture to prove it. "He got the shuffle from Fred Kitchen." Kitchen himself declared that Chaplin had taken his entire act – costume, mannerisms, the lot. "He must have a wonderful memory to have got them so perfectly in the short time that he was with me."[36] Chaplin himself said he got the walk from an old cabbie in Lambeth.[37]

---

35. No reference, Press Book 1919-1921.

36. Glenn Mitchell, *Chaplin Encyclopedia*, p.141.

37. As I examined the contradictory evidence, I longed for some comment in the margin from Chaplin. But there was no sign that he had ever examined the albums. Rachel Ford did not think he ever looked at them. I'm sure he never looked at the volumes for the period of the Lita Grey divorce; every word ever published on the subject must be in those albums, which would surely have been pitched into the trashcan if he had come across them!

18. Rohauer's Story

Not until after the programmes had been completed and transmitted did we hear the extraordinary story of how Raymond Rohauer had come to own the material. We met at his usual rendezvous, the coffee shop of the Mayfair Hotel, and a sign – "This section closed" – was placed over a whole row of tables for our benefit. For the first – and only – time in our experience Rohauer dropped the veil of secrecy and became expansive and forthcoming. He even permitted me to use a tape recorder.

When I asked who had backed him at the start of his career he pointed to another part of the coffee shop where an elegant and dignified figure sat drinking coffee. "Mr Chester, over there."

This was the story Rohauer told us.

Raymond Rohauer

In 1952, when Chaplin couldn't come back to America – when he found his visa lifted – *Limelight* was just ready for release. In November of '52, Oona O'Neill came to Los Angeles to dispose of all Chaplin's assets because the US Government had tried to attach all his belongings – his films his studios, everything. So she had to come at night, secretly, to get all the stuff out. I have to hold some of this back, to protect confidences. [The film Oona did not ship to England was intended to be destroyed. This consisted of rushes and out-takes. It was not destroyed.]

The film was moved outside of Los Angeles into a bunker. This was a relic of World War Two. You know we were always afraid of a Jap attack on Los Angeles, and these bunkers were built. They were underground with grass over them, and you'd never know what they were. The bunkers were in Fontana, California. It is a desolate place, nothing there – just desert and bunkers and that sort of thing. I got a call from someone who told me about this film being moved out secretly and did I want to see it? I said, "Okay, tell me a little bit about it." And I said, "Would you mind if I bring my attorney with me?" And I did. The three of us, my attorney, Mr Chester and I, went out there. We go to this bunker. It was kind of scary. There's nothing but a single electric light bulb on a bit of wire, hanging in the middle of this place, which was full of drums and drums of film. Maybe three hundred metal drums. This person looked kind of unscrupulous, I must say. And there was another man who had the keys. I said, "You own all this?" And he said, "Yes." So we took off the lids, and there's film right to the top. I reached in and pulled some out and there was *Modern Times*, *City Lights*, reels and reels of *Limelight* ... tons and tons. And of course I recognised Keaton and Chaplin – reel after reel. All on cores. The sound tracks were separate. And then I knew his story was true, that it came from the Chaplin vault. Where else would it have come from? I couldn't believe it. I just couldn't believe that all this was here and that I was involved in this situation. Then I thought, "Jesus, suppose we're killed right here?" You never know what might happen in such a desolate place. Even my attorney was frightened. The light was so bad you could hardly see anything.

We found a place to go and talk, some miles away in a roadside restaurant near the desert. My attorney said, "Do you have legal title to all this?" And the man said "Yes."

"Are you willing to put that in writing?" And the man said "Yes." So I still have a contract. Believe it or not, there's a contract on this. The man's name, everything is there. Yet it was like going to a fence. I've never been to a fence, but he's the man if you want to get rid of hot merchandise. Although he said he owned it, although he said he could sell it, although it was in writing, still I felt it was illegal. So then I said "What's the deal?"

"Well," he said, "What would you pay for it?"

"I can't say I would have any idea," I said. "I can't do anything with it." So we talked a while, and I sort of asked questions about the legality of it. I kept hovering on that, whether he had legal rights to sell it. "All right," he said. "I'll tell you what. How about a dollar a pound?"

"Er – what?"

"I said a dollar a pound."

I said, "Well, let me see. How many pounds would you think there are?" He said, "Why don't we go back and we'll weigh a drum. Then we can figure out the price." It was getting so dark by this time that we had to go back home, but we said we'd return the next day. Now I'm really excited. I went back home with Mr Chester. "Oh God, what a find," I said. "We have to have this film."

We went back the next day and weighed a drum. All the drums had an equal amount of film, so we estimated two hundred and thirty drums multiplied by so many pounds, and we calculated it to $13,000. It was fourteen thousand because I gave him $1,000 cash on account and I said, "Give me a few days to raise the money." And he said, "Now I don't want anyone to touch this, or anything to happen." So I had to figure out a way of raising this money. At that time, Mr Chester and I owned an orange grove of ten acres near West Covena, California. I said, "Well, look, why don't we sell the orange grove and use the money to buy the film?" Because I wasn't interested in real estate at all.

We had invested the money from the theatre in that – that's even included in the agreement, because we had to take the $13,000 out of escrow on the sale of the orange grove for the film.

We sold the orange grove for $45,000. We got a buyer right away, no problem – and we only had it a short time. We made fifteen thousand profit so that profit went into the Chaplin films.

I had to get a truck big enough to pick up over two hundred drums. It was a huge truck, and it came out to Fontana and all the film was put on it. There was still nitrate film left in the bunker – no Chaplin – and the next day the bunker blew up. The nitrate film ignited. It was caused by the electric light – somehow a spark or something caused the film to blow up. That was one day after we had the film moved.

I talked to the man afterwards. He said that he had almost lost the whole thing, because if the Chaplin film had not gone he wouldn't have made $14,000.

I was living then at 610 Robertson Boulevard. Right on the corner. It wasn't a house, it was like a complex. It had a corridor and a row of divisions where you had businesses. I took over the building as a business enterprise, Mr Chester and I. I had a printing shop in there and various other businesses as tenants. They paid for the building and I lived upstairs. I got the apartment free because they were paying for it. Underneath the apartment we put all these two hundred and thirty drums. We slept over this nitrate film every day and never worried one bit – right through the summer.

Eventually, too many people got curious, wondering what all these drums were. One day a man came in and made a crack, "If only the fire department knew about this." And that signalled me to get the film out. We had to get a truck again, move the film again and stash it in a secret place.

Now this kept going for quite a while, and we moved it to about three or four different locations to keep people off the track. It was all moved at night, too. You couldn't move anything in daytime. So I felt like I was the guy in the bunker. You know, I was suddenly doing what he was doing. I think, "What am I going to do with all this stuff? Where am I going to put it?"

Of course, I couldn't screen anything. It was nitrate. Also, it wasn't on reels. And some of it was beginning to decompose. Some of it was like cakes of ice, at the bottom of a barrel. I lost some of the film. I had to get rid of it.

And of course all the stories about Chaplin in the fifties were bad. The US Government was going to file all kinds of suits against him and the tax department was still trying to seize anything they could find. I didn't want anyone to know about this film. Suppose the Government seized it?

The next thing was to get it out of the United States. I had to engineer an arrangement to get it taken out by boat. It was moved by freighter to Hamburg, Germany. I found a place in Hamburg where I was going to put the film. This was 1960.

I met the boat. I had to keep a close watch to be sure that nothing would escape me. It was not moved in drums. Everything had to be taken out of drums and re-packed.

I met somebody from Beta-Film. They said, "We'll find a place for you to store the film in Hamburg free." I would have the only access to it, but they wanted access also. They thought there might be material of Chaplin that they could use. None of this had been catalogued yet, nobody knew what was in there. Even I didn't know.

So, ultimately a deal was made, and we had the film moved to Real Studios in Hamburg. They provided people to work with me and I stayed there for months, cataloguing all this film. It was not released by German customs yet. We just got a special permit to do this for identification. It couldn't be taken out because of the duty. It was in bond. All of a sudden I get suspicious of Beta-Film. Instinctively, I felt that somebody was going to try something to get hold of the film. I get this way at times. The true collector in me wanted to protect this thing. I figured out a way to get the film moved back to the Customs area in Hamburg on the basis that I could get the film into France, where it would be put in Beta's name, pending. No duty being paid. This was only a trick on my part, but they fell for it. I said, "Nobody can go with me. You will never know where this film is." They agreed to everything. They even helped. We loaded another ship – and the ship goes on to France. And this is where Langlois (Henri Langlois of the Cinematheque Francaise) and Marie Meerson (his associate) were helpful. We moved all the film in trucks at night to these secret places.

For twenty years rumours have been going around that I had a secret cache of Chaplin films. A lot of people have come to me in those years wanting the film and I would never admit I had it.

Langlois was very helpful, and of course we were very friendly. So we had to stop these rumours. Nobody must find out. We kept our secret a long time, but the rumours came out that I had a lot of film of this nature. A number of times, people associated with Chaplin approached me. One man was Richard Patterson, who made *Gentleman Tramp*. He met me secretly. He said he was scared to talk to me at first about this film it was rumoured that I had. I said, "No, I don't know where you get this information. I don't have anything like that". He was always trying to coax information out of me. Of course, he was working with Rachel Ford.

I tried to meet Rachel Ford about 1963. I went to her office. I didn't have any appointment. I went in and I told the secretary I wanted to see Rachel Ford. She said, "Who's calling?" I said, "Raymond Rohauer." All I heard from her office was, "Send him in." She said, "I really had to look at you. I had to see what you were like." She made some remarks about all the film I had of Chaplin. I said, "Well, I'm not trying to commercialise anything." But it was so personal with her, you really couldn't discuss it. So I left leaving it all unresolved.

She thought I was releasing the Chaplin (1942) version of *The Gold Rush*, but I wasn't. It was the 1925 version. What happened could have been very embarrassing to them, because they said their copyright was infringed on the

1942 version. I had prints of the 1925 version, whose copyright had lapsed. It was in the public domain. But my print was pirated. Every print available was taken from my original.

There were no known prints of the 1925 version. Only the 1942 reissue. I just decided to go through all the reels and make it up from the outtakes. I had a few reels of cutting copy, and I worked with a professional editor, Irvine Dumbrille, nephew of the actor Douglas Dumbrille. I found the original titles. Where there was no cutting copy, we just had to take from these huge rolls scenes that we thought would match. If you really look at it, it doesn't match. It probably doesn't match the original film at all. But no one ever knew.[38]

Then came the appeasement part. After I met her and saw it was impossible to talk to her, I thought well, why mess around with this any longer? I had the film divided up. I took all the Mutual stuff and everything and the stuff including *City Lights*, *Modern Times* and all that – that was a different lot which I put in a separate location. I then finally decided to give that to her. And that was done by agreement between Langlois and myself. I never admitted that to you, but that's true.

I didn't want to jeopardise the film – the balance of the film – because supposing that Chaplin's attorneys would get an injunction against any film moving in or out of France or Germany?

And so nothing happened to the balance of the film until you (David Gill) provided the vehicle for this to be done.

38. Most experts feel Rohauer was fabricating this story about restoring *The Gold Rush*. David Gill actually did restore the silent version and on comparing sections of the domestic release with the Rohauer version found them identical.

19. Assembling the Material

The editing of the Chaplin programmes gave us the sharpest insight into Chaplin's working methods. It was immediately apparent, however, that although he used film like water, he never allowed his cameramen to splash about and shoot what happened between takes. Every shot ended with Chaplin signalling with his hand, saying "cut" or dissolving into laughter. Occasionally, the camera might crank a foot or two more on these occasions, but one suspects Chaplin was strict in his orders that there be no waste.

While this robbed us of a myriad of fascinating glimpses of studio life, it forced us to concentrate on the work. And that, after all, is what matters. Because there is no oral history or documentation to explain Chaplin's creative processes on these Mutual films, one has to scrutinise the footage, hunting for clues in exactly the same way as an archaeologist derives history from the evidence before his eyes.

It is important to say that all Chaplin's material was well photographed – we came across virtually nothing which might have been rejected on technical grounds. It was almost all in negative form, but the laboratory work was also of a very high, and absolutely consistent standard. We know from the survival of the shop window-elevator scene from *City Lights* that Chaplin rehearsed on film. That scene shows Chaplin rehearsing with his hat and cane, but otherwise he appears to be wearing a track suit. There is nothing like this in the Mutuals. For such rehearsals as he films, he, and everyone else, is made up, and most of the time there is nothing to indicate that it is a rehearsal. But in one shot from *The Count* (included in Programme 1) Chaplin leaps into the arms of a cook. In doing so, he moves the kitchen table. While continuing the scene, he pulls the table back into position.

At the start, we were working in the dark. We transferred to tape takes in which things went wrong, or where we could make strong and obvious comparisons. But we had no shape. We had no idea how to construct the programmes.

David made the first breakthrough. Like so many important things, it was obvious when you think about it. He felt we hadn't transferred enough – I tended to cut back to the minimum, not wanting to swamp the cutting room and knowing we always had the material to go back to.

But he began joining up the shots, which were in a bewildering muddle, into slate order.

Above: Eva Thatcher as the cook and Charlie reacting to a pungent cheese in *The Count* (1916)

Right: Reorganising the dinner scene from *The Count* – Chaplin moves Eric Campbell to John Rand's place so he doesn't have to lean across Edna Purviance

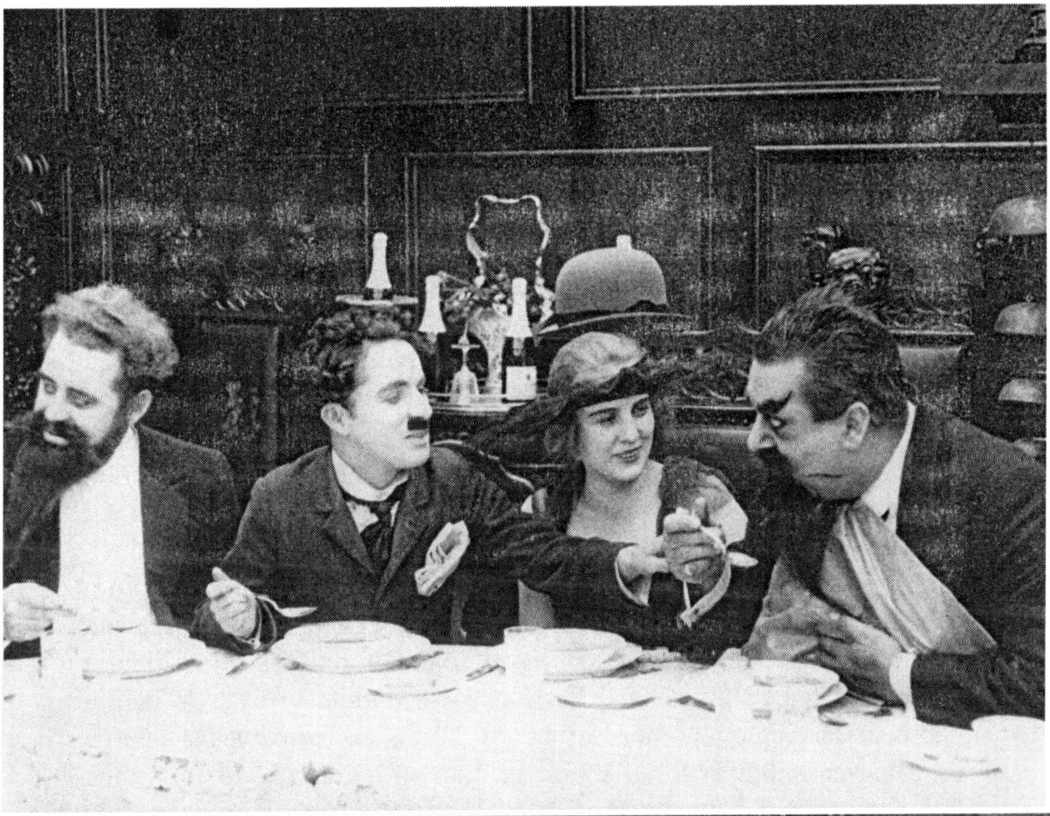

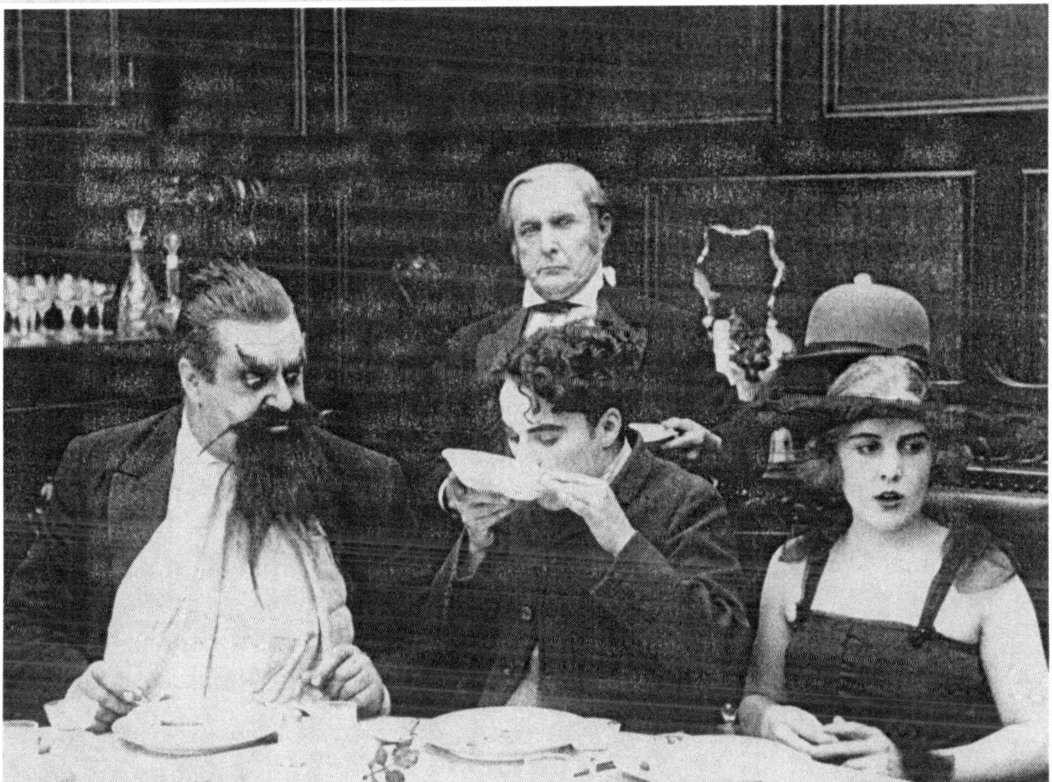

The Immigrant

He did this first with *The Immigrant*, and at once the most exciting surprises sprang out at him. He could hardly believe his eyes, as he joined slate 1 to slate 2 to slate 3 ... this classic comedy was never intended to be about immigrants at all.

There was even a shot which appeared before slate 1. How did he know? Because while the set was the same, the furniture was arranged in a way that was never repeated, and the three leading players, Edna Purviance, Eric Campbell and Albert Austin, were dressed in Victorian costume. What on earth was Chaplin intending to do? The two men are shown vying for Edna's kisses, and Austin challenges his rival to a duel. The Vevey documents revealed his plans to make a comedy set in a cabaret, in which the customers vie with the waiters for the girl. And many months later, David Robinson found a reference to Chaplin wanting to make a film set in a Parisian cafe. My guess was that Chaplin had been fascinated by the story by the English actor-manager George du Maurier called *Trilby*. (A film version with Clara Kimball Young had been released, to much acclaim, in 1915.) Eric Campbell would have made an ideal Svengali, Edna would have been Trilby, and Albert Austin one of the three artists. Parisian cafe atmosphere plays a large part in the story, and Chaplin's treatment might have been very funny. Such parodies were not foreign to him: at Essanay, he had made *Burlesque on Carmen*, a parody not so much of the opera, but of Cecil B. De Mille's film version. With *Trilby*, however, he might have been involved in the question of literary copyright.

Slate 1 shows a two-shot of Charlie and Albert Austin. Austin still wears his Parisian costume, although the high hat is not in evidence. Charlie's costume is smarter than usual, and it is noticeable that it gradually becomes scruffier through the ensuing slates. Austin is eating soup – extremely hot soup – and he burns his lip every time he takes a sip. Charlie jumps as Austin recoils; his hat flies in the air, but before the scene is over, he playfully ruins Austin's concentration by barking at him like a dog, and then dissolving into laughter. After all, it's only slate 1.

Chaplin shot that scene many times, with only slight variations. As Virginia Cherrill said, "I often thought that if he couldn't think what he was going to do next he simply went on doing the same shot over and over again until he thought of it."

Forty-six slates later, when Chaplin shot his entrance, the artist's cafe was still in evidence. Dressed in wild whiskers, with a broad-brimmed hat and baggy clothes, Loyal Underwood passes, glaring at Charlie perhaps because he thinks be looks peculiar. But this is the last we will see of the Parisian cafe. The set will remain the same throughout the picture, but the customers become less colourful. The cafe shifts in locale to America, although the waiters seem to be aggressively Teutonic.

The Immigrant is among Chaplin's best-known films. And Eric Campbell's performance as the head waiter is one of the joys of the cinema. We were therefore astonished when Henry Bergman appeared, obviously playing the Eric Campbell part. Poor Henry! One felt sympathy both for him and for Chaplin as more and more takes appeared with Bergman trying his best. We knew he would be replaced, it was just a matter of how long it took. Chaplin had some fun with him. When Bergman brings in the order, he bends down to place the tray on a table. Charlie blows his nose, and Bergman straightens up quickly, imagining his trousers have split. And Bergman plays his first scene well – he comes to take Charlie's order. Charlie is studying the menu (it's sideways – he obviously can't read). He still wears his hat. Bergman taps him on the shoulder and points to his head. Charlie thinks he is referring to the mental state of his neighbour, Albert Austin, and nods in agreement. The pointing gets more agitated, and Charlie keeps nodding, until Bergman snatches the hat and places it on the table. Charlie puts it back on again. The scene is repeated with Campbell in the final film, but on this one occasion Bergman is equally good. Where he fails is in the scene where he has to present the bill, and Charlie gives him a coin he has found on the floor. Bergman puts the coin between his teeth and finds it a dud. The audience has to feel sympathy for Charlie – they would have seen Bergman and the other waiters beating up a customer with insufficient change. But while Bergman didn't look bad as a tough waiter, he was too short and roly-poly to carry a convincing sense of menace. He did not look terrifying. The result was that the long scenes between him and Chaplin were dull.

Apart from the fight scene, which was well choreographed, the whole film seemed in danger of being a little dull. All it was, so far, was a simple cafe comedy. Charlie doesn't know how to behave. He eats his

The Immigrant (1917). Albert Austin as a fellow diner...
...and Henry Bergman in the role soon to go so memorably to Eric Campbell

Charlie's behaviour puzzles Edna Purviance in The Immigrant

beans with a knife, wipes his knife on his French bread (the extra-long loaf was a relic of the original idea) and dips his bread in his coffee. His table companion, Albert Austin, is so disgusted that he gets up and walks out. At which point, Charlie spots someone far more interesting – Edna, sitting at the next table. She is poorly dressed, and she has no money for a meal. She orders coffee.

Charlie's offer of food is irresistible, and soon she is sitting next to him. Charlie orders another plate of beans for her, and watches anxiously as she eats with a spoon. He tries to follow her example, but finds it more difficult than with a knife.

"Where do you live?" he asks. She gestures offscreen. "And you?" Charlie gestures with a spoon full of beans, and scores a direct hit on a violinist, a member of a trio playing in the alcove behind him. Another gesture hits a diner, who splutters with anger, gets up and informs the manager that he refuses to pay the bill. He is at once surrounded by a shock troop of waiters, who grab him and hold him until he meekly submits.

Henry Bergman as the Artist offers employment to the penniless immigrants

This sort of unmotivated slapstick is the kind of comedy Chaplin disliked when he worked for Mack Sennett, and it is safe to assume that he resorted to it only because he couldn't think of anything better. The threatening group of waiters was a direct result, however, and they were a splendid idea. Chaplin could now discard the mediocre material and make the best use of his new idea once he had dropped Bergman and replaced him with Campbell.

A drunk customer cannot pay the bill. The manager summons the shock troops. The scene is so much stronger that Chaplin's reactions are stronger, too. Instead of merely staring in alarm, he limbers up for what he now knows will be his own fate with a bout of shadow boxing. When he then summons Campbell for the bill, and Campbell, in huge closeup, puts his coin between his teeth and bends it like rubber, the effect is just what Chaplin was aiming for.

By a change of actor, Chaplin converts a mildly amusing scene into a classic sequence of film comedy.

As usual, there were variations in Chaplin's playing, and one scene appears to have contained the germ for the remarkable transformation that overtook *The Immigrant*.

When Campbell looms over poor Charlie with the bill he cannot pay, in one take he eats his beans and drinks his coffee in double quick time, and concludes by wiping his chin on the tablecloth. When he gets the bill, he folds it up and puts it on his head – a tiny Napoleonic hat – and adopts the famous pose, one hand inside his jacket.

In another take, he is confronted by the shock troop of waiters, and bursts into tears and has to be comforted by Edna.

And in another, he peers round the corner, terrified by the thought of Campbell's return, puts his hand to his mouth and blowing out his cheeks suggests that any moment he's going to be sick.

It can only be a guess, but we all felt that this was the origin for what happened next.

First, Chaplin brings back Henry Bergman to play a rich artist – probably French, judging by his gestures – who is anxious to paint Edna's portrait. Chaplin's original idea of an artists' cafe pays off. In the final film, the artist offers to pay the bill.

"Oh, no, please," says Charlie.

"I insist."

"No, no..."

"Oh, very well..."

Now Charlie is desperate. He waits until the artist has settled up and left a tip, and he places his bill on the same saucer. But that means the end of the cafe scene. And Chaplin has only shot enough for one reel. He needs another outstanding idea. And I'm sure he, or his associates, got that idea by trying to develop the sickness gag. "If only we were on a boat!"

It was the biggest surprise of the film that Chaplin went to the boat after the restaurant, for of course in the film the boat opens the picture. But since Chaplin used no script, and invented the story as he went along, he needed another reel for his comedy. And the boat fitted the bill superbly for it explained where Edna had come from.

The boat is an immigrant ship and Charlie and Edna and her mother are bound for the United States. The sequence begins with some very exaggerated shots of the ship lurching from side to side. Part of the effect was achieved by swinging the camera from side to side and part by moving the boat. Close examination of the material shot aboard ship failed to provide a single clue as to how the boat was moved. It seems to be higher out of the water than would be the case for such a small steamer. But we could hardly imagine Chaplin paying for a rocking machine to be installed in dry dock – and in what dry dock do you get a 180 degree view of the sea? According to the press reports of the time, Chaplin took a hundred extras out to sea off San Pedro and was caught by a violent storm, and everyone but he was seasick. But press agents invariably made up stories like that, and there is no sign of a storm anywhere in the rushes. On the contrary, the sea looks remarkably calm. The fact that the boat is moving, and not only the camera, is betrayed by the swinging lifebelts on the bulkheads.

My guess is that a floating crane was moored alongside, and by linking it to one side of the ship, it merely had to nod to provide enough movement. The camera aspect of the puzzle we did not need to guess. At Vevey, we found a photograph showing a heavy pendulum fitted to the camera head. Once the ship moved, the camera moved, too.

The rocking interior of the dining saloon we assumed had been shot the same way, but on one take the camera rocked too far and revealed that it was a set, in the studio, built on rockers. This was confirmed by a photograph we found at Vevey, which promptly disappeared and has so far eluded us. The boat scene allowed Chaplin to indulge in every seasick gag he could think of. Take after take of rolling of the boat made one queasy just to watch them. The final film opens with a scene of Charlie leaning over the side, apparently parting with his breakfast. After a few more heaves, he straightens up and reveals that he's been fishing. In the rushes, he makes use of Albert Austin, dressed as a Russian, as a character in constant danger of throwing up – usually over Charlie. While we were watching, we wondered how he expected to get away with these gags in 1917, and thought, "no wonder he had to cut them out." But in fact he includes several of them. It is hardly surprising that some people objected to Chaplin's "vulgarity". In one scene, Charlie sits beside Austin on the deck. Austin is hiccupping in a direct reference to the soup scene, Slate 1 of the entire film. Gradually Charlie is overcome with nausea, and finally rushes out of the shot. Throughout the rest of the sequence, he dodges about the deck avoiding Austin who, at one point, rolls across a hatchway, his mouth ending up neatly poised above Charlie's upturned hat.

One scene shows Charlie struggling to open a deckchair. He puts his foot through it, he gets the canvas entwined round the frame, and when he finally sets it up, the whole thing collapses under his weight. In disgust he hurls it over the side. The scene wasn't very strong, although it's the kind of thing that can tickle an audience, and Chaplin left it out of the final film. But one thing we learned was that ideas for gags were precious, and if they failed to work in one film, there was no reason why they should fail in another. The deckchair gag was finally used in *A Day's Pleasure* (1919).

Historians have noted a continuity error in *The Immigrant*. Following a title "More Rolling", Charlie is shown rolling dice, or shooting crap as they would have said in those days. Behind him on a cabin wall is an axe. During the game, or rather during an outburst by Frank Coleman as a villainous desperado, the axe disappears from the wall. Chaplin never bothered much about continuity. But he did not simply forget the axe...

The rushes provide the explanation. Charlie beats the desperado and cleans him out. He is furious, and rushes off to find more money. This is when he robs the widow, Edna's mother. He returns to the game, stakes all he has stolen, and once more Charlie wins. Now the desperado smashes up the game. He grabs a lifebelt and uses it to wreck the wooden crate they have been playing on. Charlie removes the axe and conceals it down the front of his trousers. The desperado looks around for further destruction. All he sees is Charlie – and he strikes him amidships. Charlie's expression is an eloquent indication of his feelings.

The card game contains a kaleidoscope of moods and ideas. Most of the takes end with the characteristic grin which shows how much Chaplin is enjoying himself. But one of the players is evidently a stolid sort of character. When he shuffles the cards, Chaplin stares at him in growing dismay for the man is uninspired to say the least. Chaplin's expression is an eloquent "I don't believe it" as he cuts the scene and, one presumes, shows the actor how to do it swiftly and amusingly.

At one point, to examine the hand held by a rival, Chaplin produces a prop he had never used before, and would never use again – a pair of spectacles.

Totheroh becomes playful during this scene, and uses playing cards instead of slate boards.

Coleman manages to convulse Chaplin on several occasions, either by his wild overacted rage, or by his quiet whistling as he peruses his hand. The rushes of the card game contains Chaplin's most sustained parody of theatrical overacting. We had it in the programme for a long time, and David, particularly, was most anxious to use it. But like so many other delicious moments, it had to be sacrificed to the demands of time. One young man has gambled his all and lost. He rises from the group a doleful figure. Through the door steps his young wife. He clasps her to him and confesses, and then swears by the gods that this is the last game he will ever play.

Then comes Charlie's turn. He rises from the group in exactly the same way, but instead of his wife, the tiny figure of Loyal Underwood pushes open the door, hitting Charlie as he does so. He is absurdly dressed in rags, but Charlie grasps him, and he denounces the evils of gambling, hurling the poor little man away as though he were the devil himself. And then in one of the longest takes we encountered, Chaplin parodies the Victorian morality play. The gestures are familiar – one can still see them in lantern slides, warning of drink or gambling. But as well as the stiff, arm-upraised style of acting – known as the semaphore school in Hollywood – Chaplin gyrates his whole body, and this emphasis added to the desperate urgency of his outstretched arms is irresistibly funny. Chaplin was so famous for delicacy and restraint that when he does go over the top, it is an event to be savoured.

At the end of the boat sequence, Chaplin shows the immigrants reaching the Land of Freedom. It is a sharp and savage little moment, one which many commentators have seen as political. I doubt that it was; Chaplin said he included nothing political in his pictures. It was an obvious reaction for a comedy filmmaker; the passengers arrive at the symbol of freedom, the Statue of Liberty, so the officers rope them together like cattle. However, Chaplin was aware that the scene could be open to misinterpretation.

Carlyle Robinson, for many years Chaplin's press secretary, joined the studio on the very morning that the rushes of this sequence were being shown in the projection theatre. Chaplin asked him what he thought of it. "Very funny and realistic," he said.

"Was there anything that shocked you?"

"No, not as far as I can remember"

Evidently the point had been raised by one of Chaplin's associates and Robinson's reply satisfied Chaplin. As Robinson said, "The scene was used in the final version of the film and there was never any protest about it."[39]

Chaplin worked with large groups of extras comparatively seldom. The strain of directing a group while acting in it is apparent at the start of one of the takes, where Chaplin, tightly roped in, tries to struggle free, loses his temper and shouts at the extras and at the cameramen. There is a camera flash, and the next moment he is playing the tender farewell scene as Edna and her mother leave the ship.

The link between the boat and the restaurant is of crucial importance. There could be endless shots of Charlie wandering around. Chaplin disposes of that possibility with admirable economy. In one shot, he shuffles past the restaurant, and discovers a coin on the side-

Rollie Totheroh at the start of the boat scene – 416 slates in

39. *La Verite sur Charlie Chaplin*, Societe Parisienne d'Edition, Paris 1933, p.18.

walk. Money and food become the two main themes, highly appropriate for a picture about immigrants. The coin gives Charlie access to the restaurant. But he forgets a hole in his pocket, and it falls on to the sidewalk again.

He has to reshoot his meeting with Edna, for now he knows her. Delighted to see her, he goes over to her table and they hug each other. As she sits next to him at his table, he notices the black-edged handkerchief she clutches in her hand, a sign of mourning which few would recognise today. Thus we learn of the death of the mother.

The slate number of the first of these retakes is 745. Chaplin had shot for *The Immigrant* as much as most directors would shoot for a feature, the difference being that seventy years after, very few features of 1917 are revived, whereas *The Immigrant* is constantly being shown, not as an antique, but for its undying value as entertainment.

What started out as a simple cafe comedy has become a well thought-out story of two immigrants who meet on a boat, part and are brought together by fate, a coin and a bullying waiter.

The rich artist is given an extra scene, on the sidewalk where Charlie found – and lost – the coin. He agrees to a small advance, and Charlie takes Edna to a marriage licence bureau. Considering all the headaches Chaplin endured in making the film, he deserved this approbation from Photoplay: "In its roughness and apparent simplicity, *The Immigrant* is a jewel. No farce seen in years has been more adroitly, more perfectly worked out."[40]

Theodore Huff wrote, "Sentiment and social satire are adroitly worked into the story. The entire last half is cleverly constructed around an elusive coin, in one of the longest variations on a single comedy incident ever portrayed on the screen, yet so skilfully managed that every moment seems natural and spontaneous."[41]

---

40. *Photoplay*, September 1917, p. 99.

41. Huff, Theodore, *Charlie Chaplin*, Pyramid Books, Pyramid NY, 1964, p. 70.

Albert Austin feels seasick, and so does Charlie

Epilogue

The Chaplin trilogy languished on the shelf for three years. American television displayed an astonishing lack of interest.

It won a Grand Award at the New York Film Festival, but it made no difference. It was nominated for an International Emmy and that made no difference.

Eventually, an enterprising producer at Public Broadcasting in New York, Susan Lacy, developed a series called *American Masters* and included *Unknown Chaplin* as part of it. The series was shown nationwide in October 1986. The reviews were amazing – even more amazing was the fact that the series won the Peabody Award, regarded in America as even more prestigious than the Emmy. And then it won a primetime Emmy as well.

Oona Chaplin has never been completely reconciled to the fact that Charlie would not have approved. However, she sent us this telegram, which for us was the equivalent of an Academy Award:

THE UNKNOWN CHAPLIN IS SO MOVING AND BEAUTIFUL THAT IVE SEEN IT OVER AND OVER AGAIN EVEN THOUGH THE BEAUTY UPSETS ME STOP ITS EXTRAORDINARY WHAT YOU HAVE DONE AND IM MORE GRATEFUL THAN I CAN EVER PUT INTO WORDS
LOVE
OONA
9 Feb 1983

And we found no case of Chaplin's reputation being harmed. On the contrary, when we were doing Keaton, people told us how they had been converted to Chaplin as a direct result of the series.

To celebrate the Chaplin centenary in 1989, David Gill and I staged *City Lights* at the Dominion Theatre, Tottenham Court Road, the site of its original UK premiere in 1931. Carl Davis restored the score so that it could be played live. With thousands of seats to fill across the five day event, we were anxious for enthusiastic publicity.

Alan Stanbrook in the *Daily Telegraph* attempted to demolish the Chaplin myth: "I don't know of anyone under 40 who, hand on heart, actually finds him funny" (30 January 1989). Geoff Andrew's article in *Time Out* was a vituperative piece, referring to Chaplin as "an ingratiating little runt" and decrying his abilities as a film director. Andrew's article bothered us, because normally he was a strong supporter of Live Cinema, and of the silent film. (However, he did not impose his views when it came to advertising the event and generously plugged the show.) Fortunately, David Robinson had written a splendid piece in the *Times* and there were pockets of support elsewhere, but it was all too noticeable that bookings were not impressive.

Diana, Princess of Wales, was to attend the first night, but the bookings were so feeble that Sir Richard Attenborough had to paper the house. Even then, we only had 53.3 per cent of capacity. And on that very day, the *Sunday Telegraph* printed an article headed *Enemy of the Little Man*. As I read it, I realised this was also the centenary of Adolf Hitler. The article called him "the greatest lowerer of working-class morale in history, with the possible exception of Marx, with whom he shared a determination to convince the workers that they were at the mercy of blind historical and economical forces." The writer was not referring to Hitler, but to Charlie Chaplin.

Royal premieres inevitably cause a tense atmosphere; audiences react much more coolly to the film. And our Royal occasion was disaster prone. A special curtain designed for these occasions, known as the Royal Tab, became stuck and could not be budged. The start was so delayed, we had to scrap our plan of showing Chaplin's first film in his tramp costume – *Kid Auto Races at Venice* (1914). It struck us that Chaplin himself had arranged the disaster: "I'm not having that idiotic film shown at my centenary!" Once we had cancelled the film, the Royal Tab slid upwards and we were able to start. We showed *How to Make Movies* and then *City Lights*. The distinguished audience in the Royal Circle reacted politely, but downstairs, the general public roared with spontaneous laughter. It was a heartening experience.

But the subsequent shows were a different matter altogether. With the chill of the Royal Presence removed, audiences relaxed. As Alistair Cooke said, in his tribute to Chaplin on the radio, "You cannot force someone to laugh at something they don't find funny" There was no need to force anything; the audiences greeted the film with bursts of laughter like Howitzer explosions, punctuated with applause. Sadly, the

Chaplin family had attended the Royal Gala, and none of them were present.

Despite a strike on the Underground, the audiences kept increasing. A last-minute flood of people jammed the foyer on one evening, and it was all the staff could do to cope with it. The comments afterwards were ecstatic: "I was absolutely bowled over"..."One of the best nights I've ever spent in a theatre"..."I was so ill with laughter, I nearly died"..."I burst into tears at the end"...

As for the press, David suggested we recorded the audience reaction and we sent each hostile critic an audio cassette. We chose the boxing match, when for several minutes it was impossible to hear the orchestra above the hysterical laughter.

The centenary celebration was, in the end, a great success, with the theatre packed. As we realised, it is no good judging Chaplin from a television set. He did not shoot his pictures in a televisual style, with frequent closeups. His technique was designed for the big screen, and it works superbly in its natural environment. Nearly sixty years after *City Lights* had its European premiere, it triumphed again at the same theatre, the Dominion. And we realised that there is no need to defend Chaplin. You simply have to show his work in the conditions for which it was designed. Inevitably, the new version had to be shown on television, on Channel Four. We did not expect it would succeed. But the Duty Officer at Channel Four received this telephone message after the transmission:

"I am a social worker, and I work with disturbed people. Unfortunately, my own son has suffered a breakdown. But for the first time since his breakdown he laughed. It was at the boxing scene in this wonderful film. It was such a tonic, I had to rush out of the room not to show my tears of joy."

Credits

Written and directed by Kevin Brownlow and David Gill
Narrated by James Mason
Music composed by Carl Davis
'La Violetera' composed by Jose Padilla
Title theme from *The Kid* and music for Ep 2 by Charles Chaplin
Film Editor: Trevor Waite
Film Camera: Ted Adcock
Graphic Designer: Barry O'Riordan
Animation camera: Peter Goodwin
Production Assistants: Janice Brackenridge, Elizabeth Kemp, Betty Kenworthy
Film Research: Iwona Barycz, Ian Lewis
Sound Mixer: Richard Bradford
Film Sound: Ron Thomas
Re-recording: Freddie Slade
Research: Jacqueline French, Kate Knowles
Production Secretary: Shirley McAuley

PROG 1 My Happiest Years
No interviewees

PROG 2 The Great Director
Interviewees:
Dean Riesner
Lita Grey Chaplin
Jackie Coogan
Georgia Hale
Robert Parrish
Virginia Cherrill
Alistair Cooke
Sydney Chaplin
Eddie Sutherland (voice only)

PROG 3 Hidden Treasures
No interviewees

Thames Television wishes to express its warmest appreciation to Lady Chaplin for her co-operation and all her assistance.

Also:
Roy Export Company EST
Black Inc
National Film Archive
Philip Jenkinson
Joan S Franklin
Karl Klein
American Film Institute
Institute of the American Musical
Museum of Modern Art
David Robinson
David Shepard
and
The Rohauer Collection Inc

Programme consultant: Raymond Rohauer

**The DVD of UNKNOWN CHAPLIN
is available from MovieMail at
moviemail-online.co.uk
and other outlets**

Appendix: Watching Chaplin direct (1966)

I visited *The Countess from Hong Kong* twice; the first time was in the company of Gloria Swanson, and that visit was described in my book *The Parade's Gone By...* (Knopf NY 1968; paperback University of California Press). I wrote this account at the request of Louise Brooks, who then had it printed in *Film Culture* (No 40 Spring 1966).

Arriving at 3pm at Pinewood Studios, I met David Chasman, head of United Artists in London. A fortuitous meeting; it was he who had fixed up with Chaplin's associate producer, Jerry Epstein, for me to be present on the set. He had decided to pay a visit himself. Epstein's secretary escorted us to the stage.

"I'm as excited as you are," whispered Chasman.

There was no shooting light up, so we went straight in. It was a different stage to the one they were using on my previous visit. We picked our way over wires and cables; through a door was a brilliant area of light, and some extras in evening dress were dotted around. I could hear the familiar, soft voice of Chaplin. Our view was obstructed by colossal flats – when we clambered past those, we saw the main set.

It was a vast set, representing the ballroom of an ocean liner. Chandeliers were suspended from the lighting gantries. Huge columns flanked the stage, on which played a dance band, dressed in white and playing saxophones. The set was semi-circular; on the walls were gigantic panels decorated with Chinese figures – line paintings, blue on cream. The bandstand was picked out with a yellow background; the pillars were maroon. (Production designer: Don Ashton)

Two hundred extras, in evening dress or shipping-line uniform, stood around waiting for Mr Chaplin. Chaplin was again wearing a black woollen shirt, done up at the neck, a grey jacket and a trilby hat.

David Chasman looked up at his own hat and said, "Since he is the only other one with a hat, I think I should prefer to be uncovered. That's the way I feel about it."

The camera was set up for a medium shot. To my astonishment, I saw that a line had been taped to the floor, approximately nine feet in front of the camera. That was the first time I had heard of a nine foot line being used since the glass-topped Vitagraph studio days, 1912!

There was a great deal of tension. Chaplin was obviously harassed. He was clapping his hands to a regular beat. Marlon Brando, looking remarkably Mexican in his yellow-ochre colour-film makeup, was dressed in an evening suit. Opposite him was a beautiful young girl, with an unusually fresh and charming face, dressed in a low-cut blue floral evening gown, with a pendant. She was smiling very warmly at Chaplin.

Chaplin stopped clapping and watched as Brando applauded. The crowd of extras took it up. "Yes," said Chaplin. "A slow tempo…"

"All right, boys and girls," yelled the assistant director, Jack Causey. "Remember – mild applause."

"Turn over!" The buzzer sounded twice.

The clapper boy sauntered out and held up the board: "310 take 1," he murmured, without the usual stentorian dramatics. He quietly slapped the clapper down and returned to his position beside the camera.

The extras clapped, then music was broadcast over the playback system, and the extras took up its beat. After a few bars it cut off, and the extras continued dancing without accompaniment. To the uninitiated onlooker, it must have seemed patently absurd. The silence was to allow the young girl to say something to Brando. Her voice was not strong and it was impossible to hear her.

Chaplin didn't cut the scene; he walked in front of the camera. "I think that was all right," he said, without much conviction. "Let's try another one." He stood opposite the sound mixer and stared at him, without saying anything. The sound mixer mistook this for some kind of cue. He asked, "Same one?"

"What?" asked the preoccupied Chaplin.

"Same bit of music?"

"Yes…yes…the same," said Chaplin, seemingly without really thinking of what he was saying.

He walked over to Brando and the girl in blue and talked to them. He was too far away for his words to travel, but he was nevertheless highly eloquent – because he demonstrated everything with his hands and with his body. One moment he was applauding, the next he was dancing a sort of twist. The girl continued to be absolutely entranced by him. She smiled and smiled and from her eyes shone adoration.

I guessed she was new to the game.

Chaplin returned to the sound mixer. He said one or two things inaudibly, and the sound mixer seized the opportunity to impose himself. "I'm afraid you're going to have to loop it," he said. Chaplin nodded, and this encouraged the sound mixer – a bearded man who displayed all the arrogance of the insecure. He stood up and took his earphones off and started to enlarge on his discourse about looping – but Chaplin was wandering away.

Chaplin decided to rehearse the scene. "Make sure when I say 'action' that you move across here and disappear," he said to a couple of extras, demonstrating the path they were to take across the lens. "And as soon as the music stops you come in with your line," he said to the girl in blue. "All right, let's try it."

The music came on, then it cut out, the extras continued and the girl smiled at Brando. Brando said, "I'm sorry, I can't do this sort of thing."

The girl's reply was lost in the noise from the shuffling extras. Chaplin walked across to the principals again. He was now very pent up; his habit of squinting, which made him look as if he was sneering, was becoming pronounced. He got himself ready for another rehearsal.

"All right, action, boys and girls!" yelled the assistant.

Chaplin swung around to the sound mixer. "Music!" he ordered, irritated that there wasn't any. The music burst out. "All right, stop it!" he cried. The music continued. "Cut!" he shouted again. The music stopped. More instructions. Jerry Epstein, the associate producer and personal assistant to Chaplin, had a conference with him. Then Chaplin turned to the sound mixer: "I think – how many bars have we got, six?"

"Yes, about that."

"Well, let's try four. I think there's too much music." He turned back to the crowd. "When I say 'action', that's for these two to move. When I say 'music'…"

Suddenly the music came on, and the extras started dancing. "No, no, no cut it!" yelled the assistant. I expected Chaplin to be in a towering rage, but he turned to the sound mixer, grinning. Another rehearsal, and Chaplin, though still tense, was satisfied.

Some technicians on a gantry started chatting to their mates on the floor. "It was one of those liners, the P & O jobs, well, this bloke…"

"Right, quiet!" yelled the assistant director.

"…and it was some Jamaican. Well, he'd lost his week's wages…"

"And no talking in the corner!" yelled the assistant, to quite another corner. The technician stopped in mid-sentence and glared indignantly at one of his mates. "Stop talking!" he hissed.

"Turn over!"

The clapper boy lethargically numbered the shot, the extras applauded, the music cut out and the girl in blue started talking again.

Chaplin walked into the end of the shot once more, and said he thought it was all right. A few moments later I noticed Brando standing behind me, wearing a black coat. Chaplin pushed past me and went up to him. They talked quietly and I saw Brando nod. Then Chaplin said, "You won't go away!" Brando shook his head. Chaplin laughed, meaningfully.

"He's just going to take a rest," said a publicity man.

Chaplin now conferred with the sound mixer again. "What sort of music do you want?" the man asked.

Chaplin clearly didn't know. He hummed what he wanted.

"Oom pah-pah oom pah pah…like a ship, you know, as they come up the steps. A great oom pah-pah, oom pah-pah…"

"Yes, but this scene – do you want the same?"

"No, no…"

"Well, Strauss waltzes then?"

"I don't know...Strauss…yes, let's try a waltz."

During the discussion, the tea-break had been called. Two hundred extras sauntered off the dance floor as the playback system broadcast *The Blue Danube*.

As the dance floor finally emptied, just one figure could be seen dancing – Chaplin. Still wearing his hat, he circled round with effortless grace, all by himself. A journalist next to me scribbled "waltzing round dance floor" in his pad.

Chaplin came back. As the outer doors opened, a cold blast of fresh air penetrated the set. Chaplin put his overcoat on. He was introduced to two journalists, while photographers fired off flashbulbs.

"It's been a happy picture," I heard Chaplin say. "Yes, when I get home I am very tired. I just sit by the fire and put my feet up. By 9.30, I'm in bed." He drank from a glass of iced water, refusing the cup of tea offered by one of the journalists. "No thanks," he smiled, holding up his glass in a characteristic Chaplin gesture.

A publicity girl was standing near. "Is he always as energetic as this?" I asked her.

"Oh yes, he's extraordinary. Really wonderful."

Tea break over, the extras filtered back.

They took their positions and a wild Mitchell was set up. "Put on the 3-inch for a nice, old-fashioned shot," said Arthur Ibbetson, director of photography.

Everything was aligned, the extras were ready: "Turn over!" The camera motor began grinding. "This is the waltz, I presume?" asked the camera assistant. No response. "Oh, it is," he said to himself. The sound mixer looked up. "I've got the two-step on here."

"Well, it's the waltz, mate," said the assistant cameraman.

"No one told me... I mean, what is it, the waltz or the two-step?"

"Ask Jack."

The sound mixer yelled across the noise of the grinding camera to the assistant director. "Jack, Jack! Let's get this perfectly straight." He strode across the floor. "Are we doing the waltz or the two-step or what?"

"The waltz," said Jack. The camera cut.

"Well, he asked me to put on the two-step. I mean, let's find out for sure."

The assistant director marched across to confer with Chaplin and turned back with a nod. "The waltz," he confirmed. The sound mixer put his mouth close to the intercom and spoke to the playback booth. "They have, in fact, changed their mind again. They now want the waltz."

The assistant director took up his position with loud-hailer and gave final instructions. "Ready, sir?"

"All ready," said Chaplin.

The clapper boy marked the shot "PLATE Take 1." The camera motor ground. Waltz music began, and the extras danced round the set. Chaplin surveyed the faces of the people behind the camera as well as those in front. This shot was merely for a back-projection plate to be used in connection with a bar scene.

At the end of 100ft, the camera was switched off.

The sound mixer got on his intercom again. "Charlie Chaplin's own music now, please," he said. "The Latin-American music by Charlie Chaplin."

The same scene, but a different dance. Chaplin's own rumba composition.

Then, after a long pause, the close-shot of the girl in blue was made. Jerry Epstein was called to stand in for Brando. On the first take, Chaplin made a violent gesture – sweeping his arm at Epstein to make him come in with his line. He muffed it. Cut, try again. A lot of chat about extraneous noise. The camera operator looked through the finder. "Of course, they could take their shoes off."

The extras took their shoes off and so did Chaplin. They tried the scene again. Epstein cued the girl in blue with the line: "I'm sorry, I can't do this sort of thing."

Now that the extras' shuffle had been quietened by stockinged feet, the girl's reply could be heard. She delivered her lines in a caricature of a Kensington accent.

"Oh yes, you can. It's like this." She began to do a cross between a shimmy and a twist.

"I think dancing stimulates conversation. Wasn't it Aristotle who used to walk around the Lyceum and lecture on the soul? Daddy says he never had a clear idea of what the soul was. But I do. I think it's desire. I think that's a *wonderful* idea. If you can't shimmy we'll just have to dance…like this."

(The dialogue is as near verbatim as I could get it. Epstein warned me about taking notes – Chaplin got suspicious. So I scribbled them whenever his gaze was averted.)

The girl in blue gave so much to these lines that the extras and the crew burst into a round of impromptu applause. The girl smiled delightedly. Chaplin smiled too. The tension evaporated.

A sound man atop the boom said, "I think it's lovely. I really do."

Chaplin went over to Oona, imitating the girl's accent. "Soul," he said to himself, the way she had said it – "Sel."

Chaplin's own music started up on the playback and he danced a little rumba to it, kicking his leg in the air and grinning.

"Who is that girl?" asked a journalist. No one knew. I saw a woman I thought should know. She didn't. Her companion said, "I think it's Angela Schuras."

"Skouras?"

"Something like that."

"No relation to Spyros?"

"No – but some relation to Al Parker [the agent]."

Chaplin came over and the woman, who was clutching a photograph, thrust it at him and asked him to sign. "He met you in New York," she said, pointing to the man in the picture, who was seated next to Chaplin. "He'd be so grateful if..."

I noticed a photographer frantically trying to get a picture at the moment of signing. Chaplin, looking very tired now that I could see him in closeup (he'd recently had flu) took hold of the felt pen, but it was some moments before he grasped it properly and began an elaborate signature. The man with the camera was firing off like mad.

"----ing walk all over your seat!" grumbled the sound mixer as the cameraman clambered onto the orange-box he used for a chair. "So sorry," said the cameraman, a Spaniard. At last he'd got the pictures he wanted. Chaplin handed the photograph back to the woman, and the cameraman said, "Thank you very much, Mr Chaplin." For a few seconds Chaplin looked puzzled, then he recognised the cameraman as the other man in the photograph and smiled.

Still curious about the girl in blue, I asked a publicity woman. She didn't know. She asked someone else. Still no answer.

A little man, about Chaplin's height, came on the set and threw his arms about him. He was bespectacled, and wore a felt hat and a fluffy grey coat. He was very extrovert, and spoke with a thick accent. I suddenly realised it was producer Carlo Ponti. His wife, Sophia Loren, was the leading lady in the film.

Two girls came and stood, watching. One of them, dressed in a simple green cardigan and blue skirt, had wrapped a scarf around her mouth and was idly blowing through it. Despite this unintentional camouflage, I recognised her from her eyes: Geraldine Chaplin. Ponti came over and talked to her.

Suddenly I saw the girl in the blue dress talking to the woman with the photograph. I seized my chance. "What is your last name?"

"Scoular," she said. "S-c-o-u-l-a-r. Jimmy Scoular is a Scottish footballer. Spelt like him."

"And is it true you are related to Al Parker?"

"Yes – I'm Maggie Johnston's niece." [Margaret Johnston being Mrs Al Parker.]

She hadn't realised that Al Parker had been a silent film director – that he'd been a friend of Chaplin – that he'd directed Douglas Fairbanks Sr in *The Black Pirate* (1926). She said she was very scared about her role.

"It's my first time..." she said. She looked more elated than frightened. "But he's so wonderful, so kind to me. He wants me to do some improvisation with his daughters in French. He speaks French and he did some with me. That's for another scene. Yes, Marlon Brando is very kind and very helpful."

I told her that a round of applause from tough extras and technicians was almost unprecedented. She was pleased to hear that.

"I just couldn't have started better, could I?" she said.

The assistant director called "Angela!" and she hurried back to the set to line up a tracking shot.

Chaplin came over to Oona; on the way, he told Angela how good she was. She put on her glasses and smiled her charming, delighted smile.

Chaplin stood with his wife on the sideline. He turned to her, murmured something, and they both laughed and kissed and put their arms round each other.

The motors on the heavy 10ks whirred into action, raising and lowering lights. Cables snaked from the gantries like Indian rope tricks. The camera was driven on its motorised dolly to a new setup.

On the camera report sheet, someone had written, next to COUNTESS FROM HONG KONG "Carry on Countess". On one of the camera cases was the legend PINEWOOD FILM FACTORY.

Chaplin walked over to the new camera position and yawned deeply for a full half-minute. He took off his hat and wiped the sweatband. He looked very tired.

The efficient assistant shuffled the extras around. Chaplin clambered on to the operator's seat and gripped the tilt wheel. The music started up. He peered through the finder and the camera dolly was pushed forward,

Michael Medwin, a producer who had been a comedian, and who was doing a small bit in this film, was standing beside me. I was overcome by the sight of Chaplin, sitting astride a camera platform, tracking into the crowds. There was something majestic about the sight of the greatest motion picture personality of all, behind his own camera, still active at 77... There was something inspiring about it, too. I mentioned this to Medwin, but he was talking to someone else: "I remember where I met you – it was Ischia. I saw Carlo Ponti just now – and I'll never forget the time he drove me from Naples in 1948. Italians are bad drivers, but he was a maniac…"

Chaplin clambered down and began talking to Angela. The extras were gathered round in a circle. Technicians were drinking tea. I was wilting after standing watching this extraordinary man all afternoon and I moved round the set to find the source of the tea. Suddenly there was a sound like cattle stampeding. I turned to see two hundred extras thundering towards me across the set and over to the exits, where their paychecks were available. It was 5.20.

The extras formed a long, long queue. I looked back at the dance floor. Charles Chaplin was still deep in conversation with Angela Scoular. They were alone.

Index

A & M Records 104
Above us the Waves 14
Adventurer, The 45, 66, 90, 92, 93, 94
AFI (American Film Institute) 162
Agee, James 129
Alfonso, King Luis 163
Alhambra Theatre 118
Alpert, Herb 104
American Masters (TV series) 195
Andrew, Geoff 196
Arbuckle, Fatty 163
Arène, Mme 13
Ashton, Don 201
Astors 155
Attenborough, Sir Richard 10, 196
ATV 65
Austin, Albert 7, 67, 92, 93, 94, 182, 183, 185, 188, 193
Axel, Crown Prince 23, 24

Baden-Powell, Robert 167
BAFTA 108, 112
Baker, Nellie Bly 131, 136, 166
Bali 158
Bankhead, Tallulah 113
Bara, Theda 68
Barton, Ralph 162
Baxter, John 17, 85
BBC 12, 18, 39, 111, 154
Beaton, Sir Cecil 113
Beatty, Warren 33
Behind the Screen 45, 66, 87
Ben-Hur 50
Berglund, Bo 94
Bergman, Henry 7, 59, 74, 92, 93, 96, 118, 128, 155, 183, 184, 187
Beta-Film 176
Beverly Hills 50, 118, 119, 137
Birmingham, Bishop of (Henry Russell Wakefield) 21, 166
Bishop (California) 131, 136, 152
Black Inc. 12, 13, 200

Black Pirate, The 208
Bloom, Claire 121, 126
Blue Danube, The 204
Boardman, Eleanor (Eleanor d'Arrast) 105
Bond, The 45
Book of Chaplin, The 166
Bootlegger, The 166
Bradley, David 131
Brando, Marlon 138, 202, 203, 204, 206, 208
Bristol Silents' 'Slapstick' Festival 10
British Council 163
British Film Institute 10, 16, 17
British War Relief 50
Brock, Tim 10
Brooks, Louise 201
Brown Derby 137
Brownlow, Kevin 10, 50, 89, 199
Brownlow, Virginia 41, 77, 100, 112
Budapest 65
Bunte Illustrierte 27
Burlesque on Carmen 166

California Institute of Technology 78
Calvero (character in *Limelight*) 121, 125
Campbell, Eric 31, 92, 94, 180, 182, 183, 184
Carey, Harry 55, 56
Carey, Olive ('Ollie') 50, 55, 56, 63
Carmel, California 107
Carter, Dan 38
Causey, Jack 202, 205
Cavanagh, Paul 113
Channel Four 197
Chaplin Encyclopedia 170
Chaplin Revue, The 38, 66
Chaplin, Aubrey 165
Chaplin, Charles (see Preface) 13, 98, 119, 156, 209
Chaplin, Charlie (see Preface) 6, 8, 9, 15, 17, 18, 19, 20, 22, 23, 24, 25, 27,

28, 30, 32, 33, 38, 49, 50, 51, 52, 53, 54, 55, 57, 58, 59, 60, 61, 62, 63, 67, 68, 70, 71, 75, 79, 80, 81, 82, 83, 84, 90, 91, 92, 93, 94, 95, 98, 100, 107, 109, 110, 114, 115, 116, 117, 118, 119, 123, 126, 127, 128, 129, 131, 132, 133, 134, 135, 137, 138, 140, 142, 143, 144, 145, 146, 147, 148, 149, 153, 154, 155, 159, 165, 168, 182, 183, 185, 182, 188, 189, 190, 191, 192, 193, 195, 196, 199
Chaplin, Christopher 10, 44, 65
Chaplin, Geraldine 89, 207
Chaplin, Lady Oona 13, 27, 32, 33, 39, 41, 42, 44, 49, 65, 77, 78, 89, 99, 100, 101, 112, 123, 126, 165, 171, 195, 200
Chaplin, Lita Grey 73, 89, 100, 101, 108, 131, 143, 170, 199
Chaplin, Sydney 7, 17, 33, 35, 71, 98, 110, 122, 123, 165, 169, 199
Chaplin, Victoria 10, 41, 42
Chaplin's Goliath 93
Charlie Chaplin (book by Theodore Huff) 192
Chasman, David 201
Chekhov, Anton 25
Cherrill, Virginia (former Countess of Jersey) 50, 56, 57, 61, 93, 103, 104, 105, 112, 113, 150, 154, 157, 182, 199
Chester, Christian (Raymond Rohauer's backer) 171, 172, 173, 174, 175
Christian Science Monitor 63
Church of England Children's Society 84
Churchill, Randolph 34
Churchill, Winston 33, 34
Cinema Commission of Inquiry 167
Cinematheque Francaise 46, 177
Cineteca Bologna 10
Circus, The 8, 15, 24, 37, 38, 41, 73, 75
Cirque Imaginaire, Le 41
City Lights 8, 14, 18, 19, 25, 32, 33, 34, 37, 41, 43, 44, 50, 61, 76, 81, 82, 89, 106, 123, 125, 126, 141, 150, 151, 154, 155, 157, 162, 172, 178, 179, 195, 196, 197
Cobb, Irvin 24
Coleman, Frank 189
Colour Film Services 87
Columbia University 8
Comedy – a Serious Business 38
Coogan, Jackie 15, 21, 22, 25, 27, 28, 29, 32, 33, 37, 38, 78, 110, 122, 133, 199
Cook, Clyde 78, 106
Cooke, Alistair 126, 154, 196, 199
Copper Kettle (restaurant) 152, 153
Corseau 165
Cotes, Peter 9
Count, The 179, 180
Countess from Hong Kong, The 91, 138, 201, 208
Coward, Noel 52
Crocker, Harry 8, 20, 24, 62
Cruikshank, George Alexander (illustrator) 69, 70
Cure, The 45, 71, 87, 93, 94, 95, 96, 100, 166

D'Arrast, Eleanor (Eleanor Boardman) 105
D'Arrast, Florian 105, 113
D'Arrast, Henri d'Abbadie (Harry) 58, 62, 64, 145
Daily Telegraph 99, 195
Dakar Expedition 16
Dance of the Rolls (sequence from *Gold Rush*) 149
Daring (ship) 31
Davies, Marion 20, 60, 139
Davis, Carl 10, 39, 195
Day's Pleasure, A 189
De Gaulle, General Charles 16
De Haven, Carter 155
De Haven, Carter Jr. 115
De Mille, Cecil B. 182
Denham (studios) 14, 15, 33, 76
Depression 156
Diana, Princess of Wales 196

Directors' Guild 161
Dirty Harry 53
Dog's Life, A 33, 35, 38, 53, 167
Dominion Theatre 195
Double Eagle (restaurant) 150
Downey, Robert Jr 10
Dressler, Marie 62
du Maurier, George 182
Dumbrille, Douglas 178
Dumbrille, Irvine 178
Durant, Tim 50

Eastman, Max 33, 167
Eastwood, Clint 53
Easy Street 45, 87
Einstein, Albert 151
Eisenstein, Sergei 78, 106
Elliott, Maxine 15, 22, 23, 45
Emmy Award 195
Enemy of the Little Man 196
Epstein, Jerry 201, 203, 206
Essanay 12, 45, 70, 72, 126, 161, 166, 182
European Movement 15

Fairbanks, Douglas 17, 31, 80, 106, 143, 153
Fairbanks, Douglas Jr 17, 153
FBO (studios) 142
Fenn, Lt. Clive 167
Film Culture 201
Filmfinders 162
First National 22, 70, 167
Fontana, California 172, 174
Ford, Rachel 13, 14, 15, 16, 17, 18, 19, 21, 22, 24, 24, 27, 28, 29, 31, 32, 33, 34, 37, 38, 41, 42, 43, 44, 49, 65, 70, 73, 75, 76, 77, 78, 84, 89, 99, 170, 177
Fourth Liberty Loan 45
France 7, 17, 46, 53, 65, 69, 84, 85, 99, 118, 176, 178
Franklin Circle 54
Free French 15
Free French Medical Service 16
Freight Bond 85

French Army Medical Corps 15
French, George 170
French, Jacqui 103
French, Sir John 168
Freuler, John 166

Garbo, Greta 27
Gate Cinema 77
Genesis 14
Geneva 43
Gentleman Tramp 66, 177
Gentlemen Prefer Blondes 162
George V, King 30
Geronimo 21
Gershwin, George 113
Gilbert and Sullivan 93
Gilbert, John 37
Gill, David 3, 6, 11, 17, 76, 88, 89, 120, 178, 195, 199
Gill, Eric 11
Gill, Judith 11
Gill, Pauline 11, 41, 100
Gish, Lillian 104, 108
Goddard, Paulette 51, 117, 138
Gold Rush, The 8, 14, 16, 38, 50, 76, 64, 79, 106, 119, 133, 134, 147, 148, 150, 177, 178
Goldwyn, Sam 22, 137
Goodbye Broadway 53
Gorilla, The 166
Grade, Lord Lew 65
Grand National 50
Grauman, Sid 133, 153
Great Dictator, The 10, 14, 41, 52, 76, 80, 84, 106, 107, 138, 169
Grey Chaplin, Lita 73, 89, 100, 101, 108, 131, 141, 143, 149, 170, 199
Grey, Joel 65

Hale, Georgia 50, 63, 79, 89, 93, 103, 104, 106, 107, 109, 118, 125, 134, 140, 141, 199
Hamburg 176
Hardy, Oliver 31
Harrington, Tom 72

Harris, Mildred 24
Harry Lauder Million Pound Fund for Maimed Men, Scottish Soldiers and Sailors 33, 36, 167
Harvard 154, 155
Hearst, William Randolph (newspaper proprietor) 139, 163
Hello France 53
Hellstern, Eileen (Hell) 78, 109
Herald-Examiner 106
Herman, Mr 109, 122, 125, 141
His Girl Friday 20
Hitler, Adolf 52, 170, 196
Hollywood 25, 27, 30, 34, 39, 41, 43, 51, 62, 71, 78, 79, 80, 81, 103, 105, 107, 120, 132, 157, 163, 190
Hollywood (TV series) 11, 12, 17, 25, 27, 30, 38, 41, 44, 45, 46, 49, 50, 57, 65, 103, 104, 108, 112, 122
Hollywood Greats (TV series) 39, 101
Home Box Office 65
How to Make Movies 44, 72, 74, 196
Huff, Theodore 192
Hughes, Howard 39
Huxley, Aldous 157
Hyde-White, Wilfred 29

Ibbetson, Arthur 205
Idle Class, The 38, 100, 133, 158
Ie Gallienne, Eva 126
Immigrant, The 45, 87, 182, 183, 184, 185, 187, 189, 190, 192
In the Hall of the Mountain King 100
Ingster, Boris 106
Institute of the American Musical 78
Irving, Laurence 39, 162
Ischia 209

James, Dan 106
Jenkinson, Philip 162, 200
Jesus 14
Jesus Christ Superstar 84
Jews Are Looking At You 84
Johnson, Douglas 9

Johnston, Margaret (Mrs Al Parker) 207

Kansas City 161
Karno, Fred 78, 93, 98, 106, 165
Keaton, Buster 8, 16, 17, 45, 53, 166, 172, 195
Kennedy, Merna 24, 75, 133
Keystone 7, 12, 98, 161, 166, 168
Kid Auto Races at Venice 196
Kid, The 15, 17, 19, 25, 27, 28, 32, 37, 38, 39, 41, 70, 101, 110, 131, 132, 133, 199
Kitchen, Fred 170
Kitchener, Field Marshal Lord 168
Klein, Karl 162, 200
Kloft, Michael 10
Koenckamp, Hans 112, 118
Kono, Toraichi (Chaplin's valet) 79, 135
Korda, Alexander 15
Kreuger, Miles 78

La Brea Avenue 34, 71, 104, 108
La Grande Illusion 119
La Verite sur Charlie Chaplin 191
Lac Léman (Lake Geneva) 43
Lacy, Susan 195
Lady Hamilton 14
Land of Liberty (pub) 15
Langdon, Harry 17
Langlois, Henri 46, 47, 177
Lauder, Harry 33, 34, 35, 36, 37, 167
Laughton, Charles 15
Laura 113
Le Gallienne, Eve 126
Legion d'Honneur 16
Leonard, Benny 33, 42
Les caves 165
Letters from America 154
Levy, Bert 66, 92
Lewis, Kid 66
Liberator, The (newspaper) 167
Liberty Bonds 167
Library of Congress 77

Life 70, 113
Lillie, Beatrice 149
Limelight 76, 69, 99, 118, 123, 124, 125, 126, 171, 172
Lincoln, Abraham 50
Linder, Max 15, 22, 32
Lloyd George, David 7
Lloyd, Harold 8, 9, 95
Lloyd, Norman 126,
Lombard, Carol 143
London 11, 13, 14, 15, 16, 25, 27, 29, 46, 51, 63, 66, 69, 99, 100, 108, 112, 118, 119, 120, 128, 131, 138, 163, 165, 166, 168, 169
Lone Star Studio 45
Long John Silver (character) 85
Loos, Anita 162
Loren, Sophia 138, 207
Los Angeles Times 106, 126, 141
Lourié, Eugene 106, 118, 119
Lubitsch, Ernst 154
Ludendorff, General Erich von 39
Lyman, Abe 78, 105

Macdonald, Kevin 93
MacLaren, Norman 90
Macon (Georgia) News 169
MacWilliams, Glen 106
Magnum Force 53
Malraux, Andre 47
Manoir de Ban 16, 43
Manson, Eddie 64
Martini, Florian 57
Marx, Karl 196
Mason, Clarissa 44
Mason, James 43, 65, 199
Mayfair (hotel) 46, 87, 171
Medwin, Michael 208
Meerson, Marie 47, 177
Melba, Dame Nellie 66
Merv Griffin Show 63
MGM 66
Michael Balcon Award 112
Middlesex Territorial Regiment 167
Minneapolis 166

Minney, R.J. 8
Mitchell, George 112
Mitchell, Glenn 170
Mitchell, Lisa 49, 106
MK2 (French distribution company) 10
Modern Musketeer, A 80
Modern Times 15, 19, 113, 161, 172, 178
Monsieur Verdoux 110, 128, 129, 154
Montagu, Ivor 63, 78, 79, 109
Montecito 105, 112
Moore, Prof. Douglas C. 161, 162, 163
Morecambe and Wise 66
Mountbatten, Lord Louis 29, 30, 31
Moving Pictures 33
Museum of Modern Art 17, 162, 200
Mussolini, Benito 170
Mutual Film Corp. 8, 10, 23, 45, 46, 49, 90, 95, 99, 103, 166, 178, 179
My Autobiography 69
My Life in Pictures 165
Myers, Carmel 50

Napoleon 155, 156
Napoleon 75, 99, 100
National Council of Public Morals 167
National Film Archive 67, 200
Naylor-Leyland, Lady Marguerite 65
Naylor-Leyland, Sir Albert 65
Naylor-Leyland, Sir Vivyan 67
Nazimova, Alla 142
New York 33, 44, 49, 50, 99, 100, 104, 120, 126, 127, 153, 195
New York Film Festival 195
Newman, Alfred 115
Newnam, Malcolm 87, 89
News of the World 39
Newton, Robert 85
National Film Theatre (London) 32
Nice and Friendly 29, 31
Night in an English Music Hall, A 166
Niles (studio) 126
Nitrate (film stock) 86, 87, 90, 65, 174, 175
Norman, Barry 39, 101

North Circular Road 104

O'Neill, Eugene 33
Oakie, Jack 107
Observer 154, 155
Odets, Clifford 129
Oh That Cello 117
Oscar (Academy Award) 10, 43, 152, 154, 195

Palm Springs 15, 27, 110
Parade's Gone By..., The 201
Parker, Al 207
Parrish, Robert 41, 154, 199
Pathé 22
Patterson, Richard 66, 177
Pawnshop, The 98
Pay Day 53
PBS (Public Broadcasting Service) 195
Peabody Award 195
Perils of Pauline, The 131
Perivale 87, 99
Piazza San Marco 17
Pickelhaube 41, 162
Pickfair 29, 31, 41, 162
Pickford, Mary 31, 40, 41, 162
Pilgrim, The 38, 53, 54, 76, 118
Pinewood (studios) 201, 208
Pollyanna 40, 164
Ponti, Carlo 207, 209
Poverty Row (slang) 54
Powell, Michael 77
Professor, The 15, 69, 70, 71
Puccini, Giacomo 117
Purviance, Edna 7, 23, 24, 67, 74, 146, 169, 182, 185, 187, 189, 191, 192

Raksin, David 113, 114, 118
Rand, John 98, 180
Raye, Martha 110
Reading (Pennsylvania) Telegram, The 170
Real Studios, Hamburg 176
Red Scare 21
Redmon, Granville 55

Reeves, Alf 33, 34, 79, 135, 166
Renoir, Jean 117, 118
Rhodes, Billy 106
Richardson, Ralph 84
Riesner, Charles "Chuck" 53, 54, 70, 64, 132
Riesner, Dean (Dinky) 53, 103, 104, 106, 108, 118, 199
Rink, The 128
River, The 118
Riverside Theatre 41
Robinson, Carlyle 190
Robinson, David 3, 8, 10, 13, 16, 17, 20, 71, 107, 165, 182, 196, 200
Robinson's Department Store 131
Rohauer, Raymond 17, 18, 45, 46, 49, 65, 66, 76, 84, 85, 86, 87, 88, 89, 99, 100, 106, 171, 177, 178, 200
Roosevelt, Theodore 21
Rothman, Keith 39
Rothman, Mo 12, 13, 15, 18, 27, 32, 33, 37, 39, 65, 76, 77, 78, 84, 99, 100
Roy Export 17, 78, 200
Royal Ballet 11, 120
Royal Gala 196, 197

Sales Corporation 166
Salvation Hunters, The 63, 142, 143
Sands, Frederick 27
Santa Barbara 55
Santa Monica 152
Savoy (hotel) 27, 32, 33, 49
Schulberg, Budd 33
Scoular, Angela 206, 207, 208, 209
Scoular, Jimmy 207
Sea Gull, The 16, 153
Sennett, Mack 13, 17, 95, 98, 106, 112, 139, 186
Shaw, George Bernard 52, 79, 137
Shepard, David 10, 38, 161
Shoulder Arms 38, 67, 68, 169
Show People 139
Sidney, Steffi 53
Skolsky, Sidney 50, 53
Slade, Freddie 39, 199

215

Slapstick 10, 30, 186
Smile 113, 117
Smith, C. Aubrey 154
Spanish People at Pickfair 162
Spence, Ralph 166
Sphere, The 168
Spiegel Television 10
Spirit of the World, The (photograph) 39, 40
St Louis Star 167
St Paul Pioneer 168
Stanbrook, Alan 195
Steenbeck (viewing machine) 87, 89
Steichen, Edward 113
Stone, David 77
Stopes, Marie 167
Strauss, Johann 204
Struss, Karl 106
Submarine Pirate, The 98
Sunday Telegraph 196
Sunday Times 17, 85
Sunnyside 21, 22, 23, 24
Sutherland, Eddie 8, 199
Swain, Mack 133
Swanson, Gloria 201
Switzerland 7, 14, 17, 27, 42, 43, 112

Tango Tangles 30, 95
Teddington 11, 14, 27, 32, 38, 161
Terr, Mischa 106
Territorial Army 167
Tetrick, Ted 106, 128
Thames Television 7, 11, 46, 49, 65, 76, 78, 87, 88, 89, 93, 112, 200
Thatcher, Eva 180
Thierry, Jean-Baptiste 41, 42
Tilden, Bill 51
Time Out 77, 196
Times (newspaper) 13, 39, 196
Totheroh, Rollie 23, 35, 37, 64, 90, 92, 94, 128, 189, 191
Traffic Sequence 19, 70
Tramp and the Dictator, The 106
Trilby 182

Truckee (*The Gold Rush* location) 133, 134

Underwood, Loyal 69, 74, 183, 190
Union Ice Company 148
United Artists 50, 51, 201
United States of America 7, 11, 19, 21, 41, 42, 49, 57, 65, 77, 78, 93, 98, 100, 103, 119, 136, 154, 162, 167, 169, 170, 171, 175, 183, 187, 195, 200
Unknown Chaplin, The 7, 76, 93, 89, 195, 200

Vagabond, The 87
Valentino 14
Vanderbilt, Gloria 41, 42
Vanity Fair 162
Variety 103
Vaudeville 53, 66, 92, 133, 155, 156
Vevey 16, 38, 43
Vidor, King 51, 118, 136, 137
Visitors to the Studio 15
Vitagraph (studios) 201
von Sternberg, Josef 16, 142, 153

Waite, Malcolm 148
Waite, Trevor 85, 199
Wakefield, Henry Russell (Bishop of Birmingham) 21, 166
Wanamaker, Marc 112
Warner Bros 10
Wayne, John 57
Webb, Clifton 113
Wells, H.G. 79, 137
Welsh Channel 4 7
West Covena, California 174
West, Billy 31
White, Alice ('Peter Rabbit') 106, 153
Wife of the Life of the Party 101
Wilson, Jack 37, 74, 90
Wilson, Tom 74
Woman of Paris, A 8, 13, 77
Wood, General Leonard 15, 21, 32
Woollcott, Alexander 137
Wooller, Mike 17, 49, 108, 112

World Magazine, The 166
World War One 15, 45, 67
World War Two 57, 171

Yale 154
Yegg (slang) 75
Yosemite 138
Ypres 169

Acknowledgements

Grateful thanks to:

British Film Institute
Timothy Brock
Claire Byrski
Alessandro Cavazza
Cecilia Cenciarelli
Josephine Chaplin
Marta Chierego
Paola Cristalli
Valeria Dalle Donne
David Gardiner
Kate Guyonvarch
Carol Hunter, MovieMail
Pete Kalhan, Fremantle
Andrea Lowne
Don Masters, Editor-in chief, UKA Press
Glenn Mitchell
Davide Piozzi
David Robinson
Patrick Stanbury
Omma Velada (translator) and
Michela Zegna

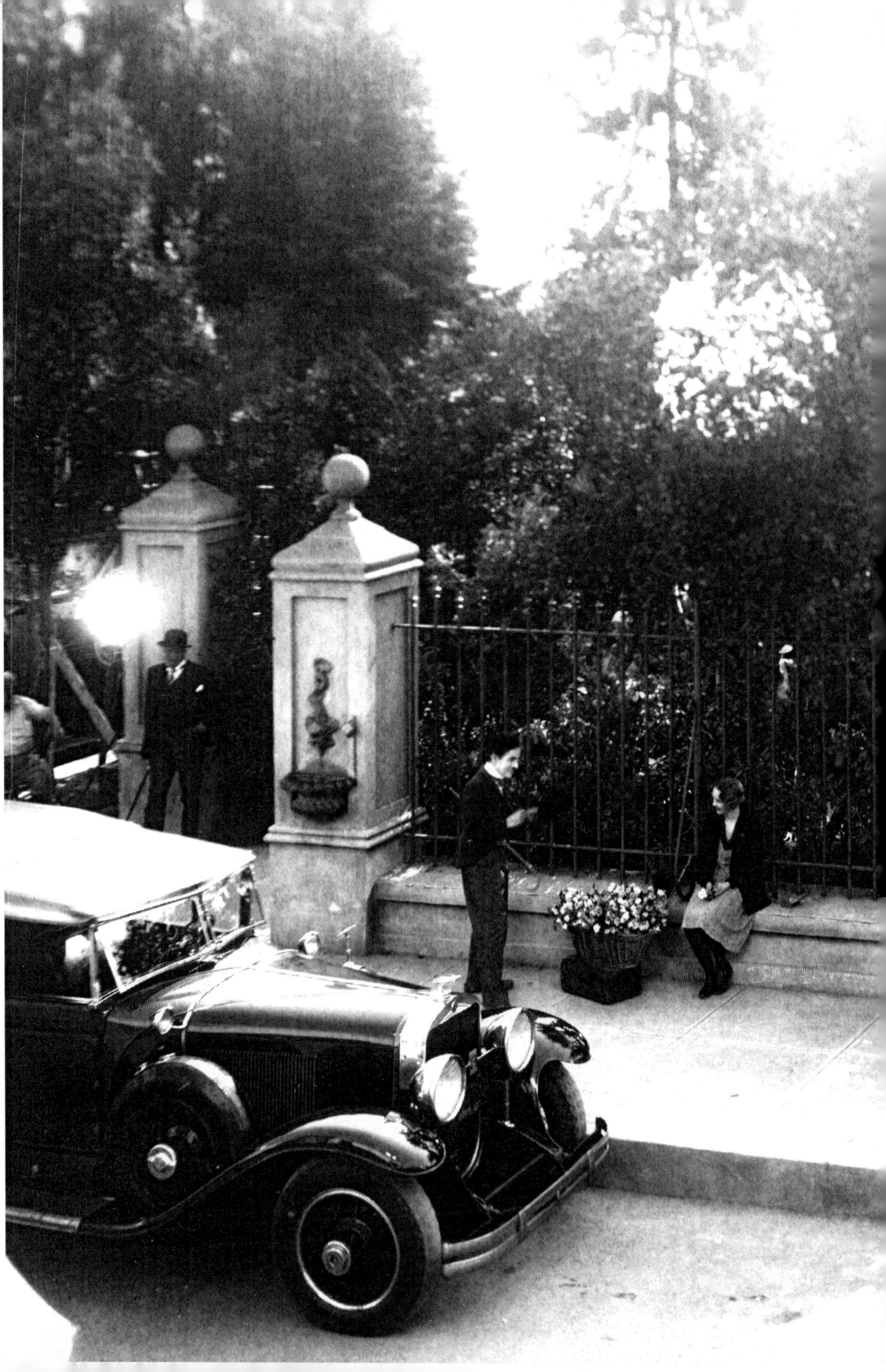

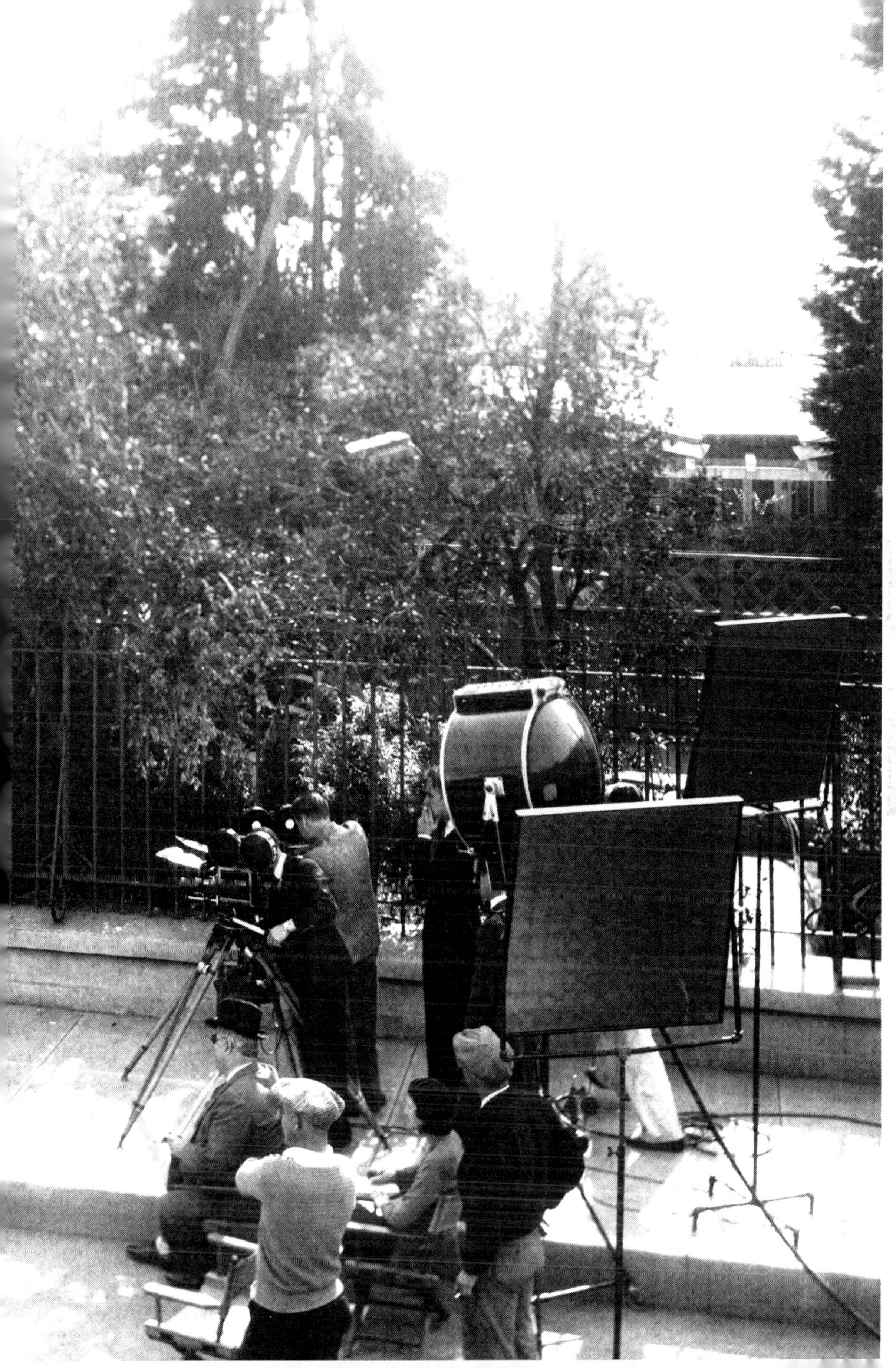

By the same author and also published by UKA Press:

How It Happened Here

Kevin Brownlow's classic account of the making of *It Happened Here*, the fictional history of the German occupation of England in World War Two, and of how the film was received by a world that didn't want to look at the way a society becomes infected with fascism.

Self-deprecating and often grimly hilarious, *How It Happened Here* is also the story of two teenagers with a dream and little else, doggedly pursuing that dream and overcoming incredible obstacles to create one of the most intelligent and chilling war films of all time.

UKA Press £9.99

Winstanley: Warts and All

New book describing the making of Brownlow and Mollo's second feature film *Winstanley* (1975), which depicts with uncompromising period accuracy an early British experiment in idealistic socialism, filmed once again on a shoestring budget and with a largely non-professional cast and crew, working without pay to turn a political and artistic vision into a reality.

Hailed as a work of genius in France, neglected at home, the film is only now beginning to receive the recognition it deserves. The book is inhabited by the same understated humour as *How It Happened Here*.

UKA Press £12.99

Also published by UKA Press:

Screen of Change
by Peter Hopkinson

His life in the film industry spanning almost sixty years, in England, Hollywood, India and throughout the world, Peter Hopkinson joined Denham Studios as a clapper loader at 16 and went on to become an award-winning documentary director/cameraman and UNESCO-sponsored teacher of filmmaking at the Film Institute of India.

A first-hand history of the moving image, and personal testimony of a man who devoted his long life to developing the art of documentary filmmaking.

UKA Press £12.99

In preparation:
THE SEARCH FOR BUSTER KEATON
HAROLD LLOYD: THE THIRD GENIUS
both by Kevin Brownlow